ELLEN TERRY AND HER SECRET SELF

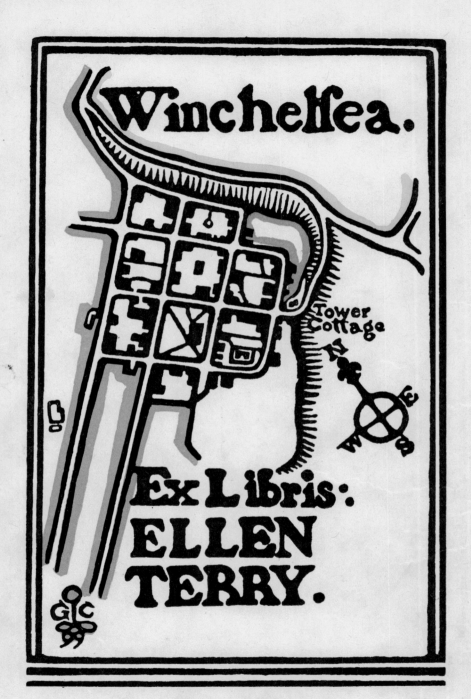

BOOKPLATE OF ELLEN TERRY
designed and cut by E.G.C.

ELLEN TERRY

AND

HER SECRET SELF

BY

EDWARD GORDON CRAIG

LONDON
SAMPSON LOW, MARSTON & CO., LTD.

MADE AND PRINTED IN GREAT BRITAIN BY PURNELL AND SONS
PAULTON (SOMERSET) AND LONDON

DEDICATED TO
MY FATHER

PREFACE

I HAD not wished to write this book.

Ellen Terry's name was already one of the most famous names in Dramatic History—no one, by writing, could add to that fame.

But it was possible they could detract from it.

And that is what Mr. Bernard Shaw, through his blind vanity and jealousy, has done: first, in permitting the publication of the correspondence between himself and Ellen Terry: secondly, in writing his apologetic Preface . . . a Preface in which he descends here and there not to salute, but to insult the dead.

He cannot help it—it is his unfortunate way.

So the thing I would have buried with that little Nelly who was my mother—her secret self—I have to bring out . . . this sketch of her—of a very small person, not a famous person—the little mother—who fought quietly and magnificently for fifty years and more to defend an old dream, and who won, though she had hundreds of people pitted against her, and among them that redoubtable

adversary, her other self . . . Ellen Terry—the
very famous person.

In every being who lives, there is a second self—
sometimes three selves—one of these being very
little known to anyone. You who read this have a
real person hidden under your better-known
personality, and hardly anyone knows it—it's the
best part of you, the most interesting, the most
curious, the most heroic, and it explains that part
of you which puzzles us. It is your secret self.

Nelly was someone unknown to all but her
father and mother, sisters and brothers, my father
and myself.

My sister never knew her, for she always persisted
in looking down on what she held to be little Nelly's
" weaknesses." She preferred to admire and to
cling to the more solid fabric, the famous Ellen
Terry, even as did Irving, Reade, Tree, Shaw and
the public.

For my part, it's Nelly that was the plucky
one—the dear one—the faithful one—and the
cleverer of the two. For always she is the woman,
and carried what she treasured most through to
victory.

CONTENTS

ANNEX

A Plea for G. B. S.

ILLUSTRATIONS

ELLEN TERRY AND HER SECRET SELF

ELLEN TERRY

A LITTLE HISTORY

WHEN Ellen Terry was born, in 1848, Henry Irving was a boy of ten; Bernhardt a child of four, and Mlle. Georges was still living at 44 Rue du Rempart, Paris. Berlin was possessed of only three theatres; Charles Reade was pottering on the continent, buying violins; and Rachel, for the second time, was sending in her resignation from the Comédie Française.

BY the time Ellen Terry was playing her first part—that of *Mamilius* in " The Winter's Tale "—which was in the year 1856, and on April 28th, and she eight years old—Ristori was coming to London for the first time; Eduardo Scarpetta, the actor, had been born; Arsène Houssaye had become Director of the Comédie Française; Irving had become a clerk in Newgate Street—joined a City Elocution Class—was about to start his career as an actor, in Sunderland; "La Dame aux Camélias" had been produced for the first time at the Vaudeville in Paris; Nicholas Gogol, the author of "The Inspector General," had died in Moscow; Rachel had made her last appearance in Paris, and was off to America; De Musset was still living, and in the Rue Mont Thabor, Paris; Richard Wagner, visiting London, had been "buried beneath the vituperation of the whole British Press, but remained calm, saying that in fifty years' time he would be master of the musical world",[1] the *Daily Telegraph* had been in existence for one year; Tolstoi was twenty-eight years old, and George Bernard Shaw not yet born.

Ellen Terry played the part of *Mamilius* for one hundred and two performances, and was never absent from the bill. She received fifteen shillings a week for this, and seems to have been praised by the dramatic critics.

BY 1862 Ellen Terry had joined J. H. Chute's company at his Bristol Theatre, in which Kate Terry played as leading lady.

Here she first met E. W. Godwin, then in his thirtieth year.

George Bernard Shaw was then entering his seventh year. Eugène Scribe died the same year, on

[1] Letter from Berlioz to Auguste Morel. August, 1855.

his way to the Théâtre Porte St. Martin. At this
time Naples possessed eight theatres. The Prince
Consort, at Maybury, had laid the foundation
stone of the celebrated English Dramatic College,
which—since it was seriously needed, and not a
speculation—came to nothing. Karl Mantzius had
been born in Copenhagen. Thierry had become
Director of the Comédie Française, in place of M.
Empis; and Irving had come to London and performed there for the first time. Eleonora Duse
had been born on October the 3rd, 1859; Brieux
had been born a year earlier; Maurice Sand had
written and published his *Masques et Buffons de
la Comédie Italienne*; Rachel had died; and Darwin
had issued his *Origin of Species*. Charles Kean
had retired, and on retiring had made a farewell
speech in which he stated that his little theatre,[1]
if fairly full, would hold £200—if packed, £250
—that he had spent £50,000 in one season alone—
in large productions given employment to 550
persons—and had improved and enlarged his theatre
to the tune of £3,000.

These facts and figures help us to realize something of the theatre world into which Ellen Terry had
come, and in which she had been at work for six years.

[1] Princess's Theatre.

B

She left the stage in 1868 for about six years—living in the village of Harpenden in Hertfordshire until 1874. Let us see what was happening just previous to and during those six Harpenden years.

STANISLAVSKY had been born in Moscow, "of wealthy parents"; Dr. Doran's *Their Majesties' Servants* had been published in two volumes; Irving had gone to Edinburgh to play his 429 different parts in about 782 days; Dion Boucicault was producing play after play in London; Gavarni died in Paris; Ellen Terry had met and acted once with Irving (1867); Rossini died in Paris; "Le Juif Polonais" was produced at the Théâtre Cluny in Paris, with Tallien as *Mathias*. Old Alexandre Dumas died, and Delsarte too; Charles Garnier's book, *Le Théâtre*, had appeared; Charles Debureau died; Max Reinhardt had been born (1873); and Irving had produced "The Bells" and taken London by storm, and followed this up by appearing as *Hamlet*. The foundation stone of the Wagner Theatre at Bayreuth was laid (1872); Mr Muybridge had made a series of snapshot photographs in quick succession, which led, years later, to cinematography; add, if you will, that the author of this book was born (1872).

In 1874 Ellen Terry returned to the stage, to work there until she became an old lady—saw the seasons passing, and the fashions—wars declared and fought and peace made several times—Kings and Queens crowned and great men and women come into prominence and pass away—and all the time, on she went at her task—joining Irving in December, 1878—and so the story of her career is told.

BUT still it needs something more as a back‑ground. 1878 is now fifty‑three years ago—half a century—yet to her, were she alive to‑day, it would seem but yesterday.

To‑day, the young men and women of thirty can hardly imagine that in fifty years' time, when they are eighty, to‑day will seem but yesterday to them: but so it will—and most of their grandchildren will be bored to death, attempting to puzzle out what the deuce this fusty old year of 1931 must have seemed like.

It seems like fifty—a hundred—two hundred years ago. Life never changes, though the years do. Inventions come and go, fashions change, prices vary, and that's about all: life is just the same as it always was, and it will remain so. Perhaps life is important . . . certainly many of the externals of life are really of very little account. Yet whether we be twenty or sixty, we take these externals to be life itself—*meno male.*

How strange to be concerned with life and not to live it—to care more about writing of life than about living it—to paint and talk life away, so as to avoid having lived—to theorize vilely without having practised fairly well.

This was not what Ellen Terry did.

Whether she had acted or not, she would have lived life: not an organized life—not the life as laid down by the religious, legal or social rules, but the life itself.

She was individual.

Intensely religious in the sense that all things seemed to her ruled by a God without human weaknesses, cruelties, denials or prejudices, she was, in the earlier part of her career, repelled by the hard and the uncharitable spirit she found in the Church; exasperated by the irritating obstinacy she found in the Law; and utterly appalled by the humbug of Society. In the end she came to forgive these things for the sake of a few people whom she loved and honoured, belonging to the Church, to the Law, and to Society.

Nelly had whispered to her something valuable to remember.

IF you want to get a picture of her times, when she was twenty-two to thirty-two, turn to the volumes of *Punch* for the years 1870 to 1880.

One has to remember that E. T. lived through four distinct periods, each marked by wars—the 'fifties, or the Crimean War; the 'seventies, or the Franco-Prussian War; the 'nineties, or the Boer War; and the Great War of our day.

The theatrical divisions are:

1. The decline of the stock system in England.
2. The development of the actor manager and historical accuracy in production.
3. The establishment of the social status of the actor.
4. The new movement in Europe.

This dividing and ticketing of periods, these dates and facts, help to make this matter seem all very satisfactory. As a matter of fact, it is a good deal mere seeming. But so would a more brilliant lie be mere seeming.

We know that no words, no dates, facts, books, can bring Ellen Terry to life; that even *when living*, no man—" nor woman neither " ever knew E. T. Then why all this pother?—why all these biographies? these letters? lectures? these revelations? Why should she have lived at all, if the net result was that no one knew her as she was—and all was seeming?

Because life protects its individuals. Life, being an excellent thing of the world, has some unwritten laws—unspoken and unseen—and these mainly to protect individuals of all kinds from the crowd.

THIS period, in which Ellen Terry was beginning life, is known to London as the Rossetti period; and 1848–1880 was a period worth living through: most periods are, but some are more so than others, especially those periods when the country is well stocked with men and women quite crazy, but crazy with intelligence, and not about things altogether material—not " get rich quick "—get to New York or Paris quick—get six daily papers, but quick—quick.

In E. T.'s early Rossetti days things went com/ paratively slowly. There was no telephone, except in the chop/houses from the dining/room down to the kitchen, and used by the waiter only, to order his " Three chops for Number Seven " . . . that's all the telephone we had then. To send a telegram was considered a thrilling business—the arrival of one might mean the coming of any disaster. No motor/cars: we had horse/buses and cabs, hansom and four/wheeler—and these were considered a great advance—something a bit eccentric, but an advance on the old coach and sedan chair.

Yet though advancing, it advanced pretty smoothly. Rather pleasantly dull, if you were of one persuasion—somewhat dangerously near the edge if you were of the other.

E. T. was of no persuasion—though to oblige, she would hold an opinion now and again. But that was no more her job, than Shakespeare's was that of holding horses.

E. T. was persuadable—especially on Mondays—less so on Tuesdays. On Wednesday, people around her found it difficult to make her understand what it was they were trying to say—but by the time Thursday arrived she could be counted on to do the very thing they didn't expect. Friday she devoted to telling them that it didn't hurt, and that they must be brave and not cry—Saturday was always a half-holiday, spent in promising her advisers that she would be good next week—and on Sunday she generally drove away to Hampton Court with Irving, waving her lily white hand.

IN Ellen Terry's theatre all the old customs prevailed; some people always arrived in time, and some were late—always late. Some people always applauded and enjoyed themselves—and some couldn't. The critics all threw down their swords and played hoop with their shields; they said that she was beyond criticism—they meant that she was the incalculable thing they had, hand on heart, too much sense to criticise.

That healed things—it helped the evening on— a critic, buoyed up by a glimpse of such truth, would go out and pull H. I. to pieces with exceptional vigour, or would laud him to the skies with the same gusto—for things which had grown grey with per⸗ hapses became positive after a glimpse of E. T. I am referring to the time between the years 1878 and 1896.

Ellen Terry met almost everyone, and everyone certainly had a good chance of meeting her, for they had but to go to the Lyceum Theatre, and there she was—now Ellen Ophelia, now Nelly Oldfield or Nell Beatrice. She played but one part—herself; and when not herself, she couldn't play it.

Like the magician Le Nôtre, who made the great gardens of Versailles, she created avenues and dells down which we looked and there she was—the spirit of her being could be seen moving in distances —forwards, back again—side⸗sliding and then closing —only to reopen some moments later. She was like the changing views in the great gardens—always

the same, never twice alike, as the hundred performances passed before us . . . she was the
foliage and the shimmering of the light on it, and
Shakespeare was the wood, the earth, the air.

She lived in a house and she worked in a theatre;
but she can be said to have lived more in her
theatre-workshop than her house.

She had worked ever since she was a child of
five or six: she had learned to look upon her work
as her life—and as the whole purpose of life is
happiness, she worked happily and therefore well.

What resulted was beautiful, spite of many
unhappy hours or days—but she was one who was
born convinced in her blood and bones of the right-
fulness of happiness and the wrongfulness of crying
about unhappy things . . . and indeed, came to
deny all except happiness. Convinced of the
goodness of loving things and the hatefulness of
hating things—kind in words and deeds about most
people, but stung to an unkind word by an unkind
word.

Only when aged did she become at all bitter—
every aged person does so—and this is what is
meant by the phrase "making provision for age."
When the heart has a day and a night in which it
fails to look upon the sea or the stars as it did at
sixteen, at twenty-six and at forty-six, then the

dangerous hour has come which was unexpected. Before that day are many dangerous days—when the heart fails to recognise a face or the tones of a voice, or to remember that it had talked things over with the brain, and together they had made, out of that stuff imagination, a false but too beautiful image of this man, of that woman, of those people.

But my mother was game, for all that, to the end; doing as she always did—to the end communing with herself—and with a final, " They are all right —it's only I am at fault," went to her grave.

Fortunate are such spirits . . . but also sane and right. Weak people are not like that—yet I have often known persons who looked on my mother as a rather weak nature. She looked on herself as wretchedly weak—so that settles it for once that she was strong. A rod of iron, no; but a tree—a good strong elm—yes.

THEY who knew Ellen Terry in the early days were sensible people . . . like those who come early to the play and book seats in time: those who came later . . . well, some of the late arrivals had spent so much energy in getting free seats that they had none left to waste in arriving in time. So some there were who hardly saw E.T. Strangely enough, these are still apt to dream they knew her better than all the rest. And indeed, a very few *may* claim to have known her latter and more anxious years quite well—but that's not quite knowing Ellen Terry. We do find a few clues to the natures of great people after they have grown troubled, and after defeat—but only a few. Sophie Arnould in her retreat at Paraclete, pottering around and writing to silly old Bel Ange, was not the same woman as she who loved the Comte de Lauraguais, and knew how to sing for Gluck and rebuke the Prince d'Hénin, all in an afternoon. And Dorothy Jordan in her prime and in her last phase are two very different beings.

Ellen Terry was more like these two than like the more redoubtable organizing type of women of the stage, such as Madame Montansier or Sarah Bernhardt. These were the strong women—one a really terrifying apparition—both manageresses born to the trade—clear-headed—money-making—independent—always knowing a trick worth two known to anyone else.

Whatever folk may report, E. T. was never independent nor clear-headed in the same way, or from the same motives, or to a like result. If Charles Reade found E. T. "hard as a nail in money matters," that is because he found her as hard as a nail in matters of money—but she wasn't. To her, money mattered very little—what was of moment was that every moment she should be well liked. Not by every Charles, every Edward, or every Tom, Dick and Harry. But by a rare few—those she loved a little or much with her heart. She loved Charles Reade a very little—but her heart told her that he was trying to exploit her—to teach her—to profit by her: so it was with Bernard Shaw too—whereas it was not in the least so with Irving.

Irving thought her a perfect actress, and so he never tried to teach or to exploit her, he just engaged her, and behaved like a true friend: that was her reason for remaining so long in his theatre, and admiring him so very much . . . which admiration she made no bones about mixing with a deuce of a lot of criticism.

She loved once, and that without criticism—only once. To her that was all that counted. Charles Reade calls her " sentimental and hysterical "; maybe she was:

> " Pains of love are sweeter far
> Than all other pleasures are,"

I found written on an old ivory paper-knife of hers —the lines almost worn away by time. Sentimental ?

> " 'Tis better to have loved and lost
> Than never to have loved at all,"

I saw in her writing—where, I forget: but is that sentimental?—I could not possibly say.

She was a true woman, and where she once loved —as she pronounced the word, not perhaps as you or I do—there was no room for sentimentality.

So much lest you go astray when reading of her either in her letters to G. B. S., or the recent Biography of Reade, or in other books about her. Take it quite truly from me that I knew her heart better than anyone else.

For I know that life of hers which can only be called her secret life—the life of her heart's spirit. It was a life carried tenderly in her hands for exactly sixty years, through every sort of storm, over every kind of road. It was Nelly's life, love and dream, not Ellen Terry's: for Nelly and Ellen Terry were and are two. The elder of the two was the great and famous actress—the important figure—known to everyone, admired by all and by me: the young one was the little girl Nelly—known to hardly anyone—my mother—and adored by me.

NELLY'S HOME—THE STAGE

I RECALL my grandfather—Grandfather Benjamin Terry—and my remembrance brings to mind the figure of a proud old gentleman—square white beard—the Terry nose, ready to snort at a moment's notice—the Terry eye, rather aloof—and the Terry voice walking by his side.

The Terry voice was Mrs. Benjamin Terry. She, too, was an actress, and some record should be made of all she did, if only for the reason that she did it all so quietly.

My mother tells us all she can, but yet does not tell us enough in her memoirs about her parents, for they who pass so large a heritage of talent or genius on to their children—giving it up to them —should be heard more of, at least after their death. They died as have died so many of those who create the celebrated ones—they died somewhat too unknown.

It has been one of my spare-time occupations for some years to trace the families of the playwrights, actors, scenographers, architects and others who became famous on the European stage; and giving at least one hour a day to this, year in and year out, for some ten years, I have in those quiet times come across curious facts. And nothing has impressed me more than the grandeur of those silent, motionless ancestors of the great figures—they who project them into the centuries, yet are themselves almost unknown.

The celebrated Vestris family, and the Bibienas, I have traced back until I came to a grandfather and a grandmother like the Benjamin Terrys, and found no record of them except that they were the parents of the celebrated children . . . that they lived and died, and there an end. It is all very well to honour the creator of the "Iliad" as much as we do, but we might much more often do more honour to the memory of the obscure father or mother who created that creator: and when we begin to venerate them as they deserve—celebrity will perhaps become rather less sought after, and true worth rather more so; and that will be not a bad thing.

"DUCHESS," my grandfather once said to my mother, "you might have been anything": and in this sentence I like the Dickens-like touch of that first word, "Duchess." It's so actorish, so full of admiration for the quick-witted little 'un. She quotes the phrase as having been said by him when she was " not living up to his ideal " of her " position and attainments."

The words—" might have been anything "—mean little or nothing, since she became all any woman could reasonably hope to become, by her own talents, by heredity, and, let us add, by the aid of the head of our profession—Irving. But it is the word " Duchess " I like so very much.

This old grandfather, if not an aristocrat by right of quarterings and azure fields and other blazonry, was in heart an ardent old aristocrat— and be damned to all democrats. To adversity— and he saw enough of it—he ever turned the cold shoulder: and while he did not become *the* actor of his age, he begat Katie Terry, Nelly Terry, Polly Terry and Flossie Terry—giving four genuine actresses to our stage—and then he gave it a younger son, Fred Terry—a genuine actor. Besides these five, he had two more sons, George and Charles Terry, who devoted some thirty to forty years' service to theatrical management . . . so, taken all in all, I think that Benjamin Terry and his wife deserve to be remembered, for it seems to me that their theatrical record is a high one. Seven children all devoted to one calling is a good thing to have given any nation.

NELLY TERRY[1] was never by persuasion what is called "respectable," and nobody is so by nature.

All the Terrys were not a little Irish; but, spite of their Irish swing, they one and all did their best to capture the English stroll, and some managed to do so pretty well, avoiding the English strut.

Each had his or her own characteristics—though Nelly, Flossie and Fred were very much alike in their buoyancy and . broad-minded outlook upon life and persons, and their generosity when it came to acts. Nelly Terry was probably the most self-willed of them all—a little naughty— though I feel that Fred when a young man ran her

[1] It seems to me rather important that when I speak of my mother I shall refer to her sometimes as Nelly, sometimes as Ellen Terry, and sometimes as E. T. She was these and other names to herself—and I think some women mean a very great deal when they sign themselves one way and very little when another way. E. T. would often sign her letters with the name of the part she was playing—" Your loving *Ophelia* " . . . Whether this was an old stage custom, or whether of her inventing, and whether it spread very far, I do not know, but I have one or two letters from Irving, signed *Benedick*, and one addressing me as *Dear Count*, when about to play in " The Dead Heart." E. T. sometimes signed herself *Ellaline*, the part she played in " The Amber Heart "—sometimes *Beatrice*—sometimes a mixture of home name and theatre name. I suppose for a time I must have caught this trick, for I see that in a letter to Sir William Rothenstein, written when I was studying Shelley's " The Cenci," I signed myself half stage, half home name.

To Violet Vanbrugh, E. T. was always *Camma* (" The Cup "), and to this day Violet Vanbrugh never speaks of her to intimates by any other name. To Sir Albert Seymour (" Bertie," or " The Bart," she called him) she signs herself *Cicely* as a rule ; but from what play this can come, I have not the faintest idea.

c

pretty close: the two were really very alike for big-heartedness, shrewdness, and impulsive actions. It is the stuff which makes for strong English actors.

Marion was the gentlest and the least ambitious, Ellen and Florence the cheekiest and Kate, perhaps, the shrewdest. If gentleness, nobility, and freedom from ambition were qualities sufficiently valued on the stage, Marion would have outshone all the rest, for Kate retired early in her career. It's cheek you need, to get on in any branch of life— cheek plus genius—and Ellen had plenty of that, and Flossie had some of it.

Florence Terry (a wonderful nature about whom not half enough has been written) married happily, and so did Kate, but Marion married not at all. Kate married Mr. Arthur Lewis—Flossie, Mr. William Morris—but not until well past twenty—and both settled down and were " happy ever after."

Now Ellen, being too obstreperous, somehow or other never was " happy ever after " in the same sense—she wasn't born to be that, and so much for bad luck; but she became the most famous of all the family—and so much as compensation.

I have been sometimes amused to hear folk saying, " Ellen Terry never thought much of the other members of the family."

So I will quote from three letters we received in Rapallo, in—I think—1921–22, though I see no dates of any year:

March: I saw Fred, by the way, play *Benedick* a few weeks ago—it was such a treat—he was *quite grand*, and it was strange that all the tosh he has been soaked in all these years hasn't affected his style—his method was excellent.

October 28: . . . Phyllis speaks in interview I am told of wanting *eventually* to play *Lady Macbeth*—at present she is doing *Trilby* on tour. . . . There's *no one* can *touch* her you know and she had a grand reception at the Coliseum and she made A SPEECH.

"Bless you—it is just ripping—gorgeous—to be back home again."

March 8: . . . Katie Gielgud has exceedingly clever boys— *one* of 'em, Jack, is devoted earnestly to Ted and all his works—I read him the chapter in Ted's book (*The Theatre Advancing*) upon Imagination—and it fired him off—I've little strength or time or I'd see much of him.

The eldest boy (very clever too) has just married . . .

SHE was married far too early—she was but sixteen years old—and that would never do— and so a separation followed soon after, and she ran off with someone she loved, and whom she loved till she died.

She was the Bohemian of the Terry family, and the family spoiled her with their affection—and I know how she loved them all in return.

All were in one way or another like their
father and mother—my grandfather and grandmother—two beings who were stage king and stage
queen makers, and therefore must have been a bit
Imperial.

But they made Ellen Terry not only a queen of
the stage, but a good rebel too—it was probably
that which ensured her ultimate victory. E. T. was
certainly rebellious—she scorned respectability,
despised all sorts of sensible things, rode life like
one of the wildest of Amazons—always taking
leaps in the dark—surmounting difficulties rapidly
and easily—but for ever preaching what she did
not practise . . . a conundrum, a success and a
glory of the English stage.

She hated the conventional, and what a blessing
that she did so. It wasn't that she couldn't be
conventional—it was that she hated being so,
because it seemed that being so would be to her
all a sham.

And you would have thought that an actress
would adore and play up to any sham—the artificial
in life—since the whole of acting is shamming, and
the actor a hypocrite[1]: and indeed, if Nelly had not
been so very much what she was, she too would have
done this.

---

[1] The word " actor " in Greek signifies " hypokrites."

What was she? She was first and last an actress, born in the Theatre, who loved that land of her birth so devotedly—so passionately—that she never associated it with the word "sham." Its life was the real life—whereas life as lived in houses was to her the sham life . . . and so she said to herself when she was very young, and so she went on:

"It's all such sham there, sham—cold—hard—and pretending: it's not sham here in our Theatre—here all is real, warm and kind—we live a lovely spiritual life here. And when the curtain rises, I go in and out of Athens, Venice or Messina—or along the old London ways of Wolsey's time—here, on this glowing stage, I meet the great people of the Earth: to-day King Leontes and his lovely Queen—to-morrow the wicked King John: but what a lovely voice he has, our King Charles John Kean, and how kind he is to us all—to Mother last Friday . . . how he helped her——"

and here Nelly Terry's eyes filled with tears of joy at the remembrance; but only because the heart was too full were the eyes called in to nelp things out.

Nelly was all imagination, all feeling, and all in a dream. And on this sensitive nature, on these feelings, the big and vibrating lines of Shakespeare played—the world behind the scenes lent colour and actual warmth to the whole illumination that came to her, and she was sworn once and for ever to the stage.   Later, we shall see that she left it, as she thought, " for once and for ever."

LIKE Nance Oldfield, Ellen Terry had genius; and genius is a curse or a blessing to the possessor, according to the direct use to which he can put it. A merman with a genius for making trousers would suffer.

You can't pick and choose about a curse of that kind—you can't say " I will now become a genius," or " I have decided never to acquire genius "— for it is not acquired—you are, fortunately or unfortunately, born with it. It can be a blessing, but it is more often a curse.

Genius has to fly free—talent chooses to go on rails: talent arrives at its destination, and within scheduled time—genius seldom has a destination; it arrives somewhere all the time, because it is obliged all the time to be leaving somewhere. So, talent is able to move to a fixed rhythm, and makes for a given spot, and does things: genius is for ever changing its rhythm, goes nowhere, and *is* something, in distinction to *doing* something. The combination of the two—Shakespeare and Burbage—produces such valuable results that in an age where genius is too often wasted, and talent driven to seed too soon, it would be no bad thing were the two to be more often brought together—it would show some sense of economy.

Ellen Terry showed inspiration early. This inspiration is not a thing which it is possible to acquire. It comes quite often to the helpless: it sometimes succours, and it sometimes kills.

If some little actress or danceress be truly lost— quite desperately helpless—lost and entangled in the thing she loves more than herself—it is then that inspiration is sent to her by the Gods—and the Gods only help the helpless. From the clever, the able and the self-possessed, the Gods have a sly habit of drawing back, and slipping past them. These Gods, pulling on their white kid gloves, are always in a state of fun, and nothing excites their laughter so much as to see the self-contained little miracles of important men and women, squeaking, grimacing, strutting up and down—and feeling . . . sufficient for the day. Doing it all so ably, so excellently, and yet indeed a trifle smug— admirable, but so dull: attracting the attention of a thousand nobodies—these by their thousands telling to others and to more and more the less and less that their idols have done: with cries of " Oh " and " Ah," they grimace their admiration of the little actor; without pause they clamour on

about these dull clever ones, these idols of the
public.

But the chosen of the Gods, for a long time, gets
passed over by the world—no one says a word: and no
one said much about Nelly. She looked a little too
wistful and thin—looked fearful—one hardly hears
her—one is listening to so many others. So she gets
cast aside, this true worshipper, this devout servant
of the stage—stands helpless—all her self given away
to it, she no more exists.

Nelly Terry, till she fell in love, would be in the
Theatre longer than anyone else; she would escape
to it to be warm and happy there—running in
through the stage door or the pit door or the big
doors which were gilt and lighted up—but at all
costs and anyhow into the place which to her was
all Heaven—lovely—Home!

NELLY STAMPS HER FOOT

ONE day Nelly stamped her foot and flung theatre and friends away for the worth‑while thing. Nelly was in love. In 1868 came this change: she was truly in love, and she left the stage for six years, and she writes in her memoirs:

"I had no intention of ever acting again when I left the Queen's Theatre. . . . I left it without regret. I was very happy leading a quiet domestic life in the heart of the country. When my two children were born, I thought of the stage less than ever. They absorbed all my time, all my interest, all my love."

As is usual, I believe, with young mothers, and my mother was twenty‑one when my sister Edith was born. Still, the three "alls" is something of an exaggeration, since she must have had some time, interest and love left over to give to our father. I cannot think that she was one of those donkeys who, on the birth of their children, turn sweetly to the father and say: "I only loved you so that I might have children—do you mind?"

WE had a house in the country, at Fallows Green, just out of Harpenden, which had been built for us by our father. Nelly liked children, and so she liked me and my beautiful little sister Edy. Edy was dark; I had white hair, and I have white hair still.

My little sister was just about two years older than I, and she was not an obstinate child—she had a will. I had no will—I was merely an obstinate child. Our mother could note the difference immediately.

A young female cub with a will of its own was a positive threat to her—a kind of visitation from heaven—a mother would have to look out: whereas a merely obstinate male brat could be easily managed, more especially when a mother soon realized that this brat's stomach was one of its weak spots—give it some pudding, and it would become docile. Give the female six puddings, and the mighty will would dash all six to the floor and demand its rights.

"Great God," whispered my mother to the two walls of the narrow passage up which she fled, "What on earth am I to do when off she goes again!"

It never dawned on the dear mother what she was to do: but one thing she would not do, *that*

About 1870

ELLEN TERRY

pencil sketch by
Edward Godwin

she already knew—she would never attempt to get the better of the girl . . . but not being at all frightened of the boy, that lump of iniquity who liked food, she decided that she *would* train him— and no one else should. Both of these decisions were glorious errors of judgment, for all children can take advantage of mothers.

THIS was in those early days at Harpenden. But I do people suppose that Ellen Terry, possessed as she was of a unique and driving genius for acting Shakespeare, would allow Nelly to stay for ever down in the pretty village of Harpenden, humouring a little girl and training a little boy? Mothers as a rule can hardly do better, but in my mother's case there was the genius of E. T. to consider, was there not?—and this fact it is which makes her case an exception to the rule—does it not?

When a man or a woman has a fiend of a talent in tow, it often becomes a case of Sinbad and the Old Man of the Sea. Sinbad managed to kill the old man, and if you don't want your talent to stifle you and wreck the life of your life, you must kill it too.

And Ellen Terry had this talent very strongly in her: so strong it was that it amounted to genius— and of genius they say in Italy, " Oh ! Bene, bene

—male, male." Yes, good, good—very good—but alas, bad, bad—very bad. A blessing to the world, a curse to the possessor of it: for genius is something so mobile—it fidgets in a man or a woman—it is a restless thing, not greater nor lesser than most other things, but so different: and when it takes up its abode in a physique and a mentality not quite strong enough to hold it steadily, it shatters.

Unbalanced artists are like old sailing-ships, in which, when loaded carelessly, the bales of silk and the boxes of ivory tusks and gold ingots, and the rest of the freight, would all begin to roll around at the first storm. Then the wits must scurry and quickly lash things down. Often a boat came through to port safe and sound, but others floundered and were sunk.

Nelly's physique and good sound sense served her genius well. She was well balanced—but she had to do as her genius dictated. Her motherly instinct would have made of her the mother of a large family—that instinct would have seated her in a large chair, in some old-world house which she would have directed perfectly, just as many a noble lady does to-day. She would have grown old, kept slim, not grown tired—just become old, serene, and ever wiser and wiser—teaching her children and grand-children how to rid themselves

of their egotisms, bestowing on them all the exper,
ience gained by meditation and observation, devoting
all her time and powers to them—never acting . . .
living.

That is what Nelly longed to do: and her genius
—E. T.—would not let her.

Hers was quite another fate: she was destined
to act—forced to give two,thirds of her life and
time to the public for whom her genius was intended.
That she accepted this destiny in the right spirit,
and went forward gaily and without hesitation, is
the important thing.

Life and work are apt to clash, with certain people
—they almost always do with artists—and when
those people feel a distinct call urging them to
sacrifice the one or the other, it generally ends
more or less in the destruction of all that really
counts so far as the life is concerned. They give
up life for the sake of that which they feel called
to do, and it is never easy to be giving up life,
whatever it may be for.

I think it is probably a great delusion; for I
believe, with many others (whether that is with the
majority, I don't know) that life is the important
thing, and work, whatever it may be, is secondary
. . . though I myself have, like my mother,
always, for some reason, felt the call to work greater

than the call of life. I do not mean the practical call to work from a desire to make money, though I would not be so stupid as to underrate the value of money, as a result of work, when it comes.

I touch on this because I do not mean by " work " primarily a means of making pounds, shillings and pence. I mean that itch to work, that attraction towards some special work and no other work, that seeming indifference to other people's feelings when working, because of the concentration necessary to the work.

The actor and actress, having to appear in a certain theatre at a certain time, in a certain play, with certain other people, for a public waiting for the curtain to go up—everything has to give way before this work.

NOW my mother had to do like everybody else in this, if she was to be an actress. But the attraction life had for her was very great.

She had all the sensitiveness of those who love what is beautiful in nature, in the rising of the sun and moon and the going down of these, in the wind, in the sea, in the changes of light, in the fresh air, the trees and flowers growing in the woods and lanes, old castles and cottages, rivers, people, books, pictures—and *time* to enjoy all these things. And then her house in the country—the house at Fallows Green, Harpenden, in which we all lived, I mean, for no other house was ever quite the same to her as that one.

All this proved to be not merely an attraction which drew her away from the theatre, but a reality which rendered the theatre positively ridiculous.

What, after all, is this hectic business of going out as it gets dark and entering a theatre and pretending to be somebody whom you are not, and hearing people yelping in front, and feeling their emotional love come back to you with their shouts of "Bravo! Bravo!" What does this really amount to by the side of life itself, as my mother was living it at Harpenden.

And yet our family—the Terry side of it, has always put work before anything else, and always there has been for us that fatal attraction to the theatre. It could be relied upon at any moment to act on any of us, and bring us to task as pins fly to the magnet. Was it a thing to resist? I am sure I don't know. All I know is that it is irresis, tible, and has always been so to us.

Here was my mother, living happily down in Har, penden; we read in her book of her contentment

there—of the days of happiness, the hours of joy,
the delight it was to her to see the flowers—to
hear my sister Edy saying, " There are lots more."
We realize that she was tingling with the joy of
what is called " real life": and then that strange
creature, that meddlesome old Charles Reade (pos،
sibly one of the worthiest of men, but to whom
I bear a grudge which I am sure will never grow
less) comes leaping over the hedge in a scarlet
coat (for it appears he was hunting), and, like some
ludicrous Mephistopheles, tempts her back to the
stage with an offer of forty pounds a week. . . .

Forty pounds a week in exchange for dear life!

" Where have you been all these years ? " he
asks.

" I have been having a very happy time," answers
my mother.

" Well, you've had it long enough " (what a fool
of a phrase !) " come back to the stage."

" No, never ! " she says—life for a moment
flaring up with all its proper, ordinary aspect of
downright commonsense and courage.

" You're a fool ! " replies this comic Mephis،
topheles, " You ought to come back."

And then my mother says something that I do
not believe to be utterly without a flavour of untruth.
She says:

"Suddenly I remembered the bailiff in the house a few miles away, and I said laughingly: 'Well, perhaps I would think of it if someone would give me forty pounds a week!'

"'Done!' said Charles Reade" . . . why, it is almost like the words out of "Faust"—one expects to see a flash of red fire . . . "'I'll give you that, and more, if you'll come and act in my play.'"

And she accepted.

What I think is something not exactly like the truth and nothing but the truth, is that she "remembered the bailiff in the house."

I think the truth is that she remembered the stage, and had all at once felt the full force of the pull of that damnable magnet, the theatre, which had been attracting her from a great distance for the last two years.

For have we not all known men and women who have had bailiffs in their houses; who have not had any money, and who had some children; and have we not known them to see it through, come what come might, and not go back to any old theatre, not return to any Diplomatic Service, nor go off to sea? We know of such people now, and we shall know of them centuries from now.

But this has to be said—that it is far harder for those whose work draws them as the theatre draws

D

an actor, and as the sea drags a sailor . . . it is far harder for these to resist that pull, and all the promise it seems to hold.

Thousands of men are so obsessed with this notion of the efficacy of work, that they become oblivious of life: then they pinch up life, so as to make it small and force it to fit in with the work. The ideal, of course, is the other way round—to swell out work to the size of life—and some people are able to do that.

I REALLY do not understand why, after all these years, I should dislike the thought of Charles Reade so much. It is not the man that I am furious with, it is the dramatist; not a very great dramatist and far too easily convinced of the efficacy of his work—this odd chap looking out for a good actress to play parts in his plays, and thus make them successful.

What a pitiful lack of true friendship he showed, at this moment in this young woman's life—how reckless this horsed hedge-leaper, with his too quick and ready solution to a problem both sensitive and difficult, yet soluble by a true friend who could find time and thought to give to it !

How often is this same story going to be repeated, at the expense of very dear life ? For Charles Reade

was not in any special theatre which he had made
into his home, into which he might have invited
Ellen Terry and a dozen more talents, and made a
home for them, so that they could be at rest and
worry no further about these jokes called bailiffs—
nor even critics—nor impresarios. Nor was he
calling for recruits to a grand, if losing cause.

Well, anyhow, Nelly was already sorry she had
stamped, as she turned her head towards Fallows
Green: but E. T. wasn't a scrap sorry . . . rash as
ever, she it was who stamped this time, and turned
from Harpenden, and took Nelly with her towards
the ten times more precarious possibilities offered
her by the vague and capricious Reade—and ran
at them with her eyes shut and her hands out.

ENTER HENRY IRVING

NELLY FLIES OUT OF THE WINDOW

ARRIVING in London, Nelly looks around her in dismay. As well she might—for had Reade slain the bailiffs—paid them off—routed them?

Not a bit of it—what he had done was to offer her a very flimsy uncertainty. She knew that; and after she had done all she could for Reade's play, "The Wandering Heir," which report says she played gloriously, he seems to have done very little for her—for "things were at their darkest," she writes, a year later.

Forty pounds a week for a few weeks won't go very far. If we drop talking of life and of art and come to business, what we want is anyhow a sure living all the year round. That obviously never occurred to Charles Reade, the playwright, and later on it does not seem to have occurred to George Bernard Shaw: just look at the *Correspondence between E.T. and G.B.S.*, and you will see what I mean.

What did occur to Charles Reade was that here was a good opportunity to launch his propaganda plays with a good actress to inspire them, and to make a nice big profit out of the play and Ellen Terry. The profit is a thing Mr. Shaw would never have considered, but for the rest he was quite like Charles Reade.

What a life—bailiffs on the brain—on Reade's brain . . . she gets to London, and in every shadow terrors seem to lurk. Bailiffs to right of her—bailiffs to left of her seemed to volley and thunder at her.

She flees down Tottenham Court Road. Heavens ! —this man coming towards her ! . . . Charles Reade !——

" I thought you were a bailiff ! "

" My dear child," says he in a hoarse whisper, " have you—have you such a thing as half⸱a⸱crown about you ? "

" Of course ! " cries Nelly, producing dozens of them, and thrusting them onto the impecunious Reade.

" Here," says Reade breathlessly, " here is the contract—forty pounds a week—but not till the end of the month.

" I am so worried with bailiffs," says he, looking for sympathy—and getting it—" Sheridan and I seem to be alike in so many respects. Have you been to any plays, Nelly, since you got back to town?"

"No, but I want to see Mr. Irving act."

"Irving . . . Irving . . ." says Reade—"let me see—Irving? Oh, *Irving!* No use going to see that fellow—a useless rascal—without a spark of intelligence—worst actor in London—damn brutal to his poor dear wife—helpless idiot, any-how."

"But I should like . . ." begins Nelly.

"LIKE!" thunders Reade—"You should Loathe —Loathe—L o a t h e ! ! !" and off he goes, leaving her standing in Tottenham Court Road . . . London.

AND that is about all he did do. He had dragged her up by the roots from the country soil, and had brought her to town, but he never really held her up, and soon she left Reade and his work, and was next year seen at the Prince of Wales' Theatre, acting for the Bancrofts in "The Merchant of Venice," described by Beerbohm Tree as "the first production in which the modern spirit of stage management asserted itself, transporting us as it did, into the atmosphere of Venice, into the rarified realms of Shakespearean Comedy" . . . "Since then," he proceeds, "no doubt millions have flocked to this class of production."[1]

So that Charles Reade's coat wasn't scarlet after all —it was but pink: and his entry in his notebook about her, and his sudden descent on her at Harpenden, are unconvincing, and only typical of that fluffy Bohemianism which reigned in the theatre of that time, and had ruined it.

The men who stopped it were Bancroft, Hare and Irving, who had the respect for the stage necessary to lift it from the casual condition of happy-go-lucky into a solid and sensible position amongst the other professions.

ELLEN TERRY, after acting *Portia* for the Bancrofts, and some other parts, passed to the Court Theatre, well directed by John Hare. She played several seasons there, from 1876, acting in a play called "Brothers," (November 4th), then in "New Men and Old Acres," (December 2nd), which she says brought Mr. Hare £30,000—in those days a good sum for a little theatre to book . . . then in "The House of Darnley," (October 5th, 1877), and finally—March 28th, 1878—in "Olivia."

He doesn't describe Charles Reade's efforts, spite of Reade's production of "Rachel the Reaper," in which he introduced "real pigs, real sheep, a real goat, a real dog, a real wall of real bricks, and had real litter strewn all over the stage." E. T., *Story of My Life*, page 87.

By this time she had no longer quite the same fear of bailiffs which Reade had managed to instil into her by his unnecessary panicking: but they might have broken out at any moment; and though at this time (1876) she married Charles Kelly, he seems to have got no nearer than did Charles Reade to the solution of the problem: " How positively to cure Bailiffry ? "

Everyone is in a panic . . . enter Henry Irving, and the problem is solved !

It is Irving who, in a brief note of three and a half lines—twenty-eight words, in fact—asks if he may have the pleasure of calling upon Miss Terry at two o'clock, and then and there gives her a permanent home for the next twenty-four years— a continual warding-off of a world of possible bailiffs and over-eager dramatists—and that freedom from worry that every actor and every actress longs for, so that they can do their work properly.

His was the only practical proposition: all those other people were like the theatres and their impre-sarios of to-day—inviting actors to take up what they recommend as " a very good thing for them," and play in such a part for three weeks at His Majesty's Theatre, in another for six weeks at the Duke of

York's, another for six weeks at the Apollo, four weeks again at the Savoy. What sort of life is that? —a very bad one, surely: and what sort of good work can be done in such bad life?

AND then the Gods move mysteriously, and going around about to help her, enter her being; and slowly she becomes Ellen Terry—still innocent of what she is becoming—still with but one passion, the boards of the stage—still helpless but devout—humbler than anyone else, even when she rises higher than the rest—a little distraught— smiling, though, with joy, so that we wonder what it is in that face—its double look: and then, saying she can hardly believe it, she believes . . . at thirty years of age—" It's true—it's true ! " she cries.

She is the greatest actress of Great Britain; but it wasn't *that* she meant. What she meant was, " The promise—the voices promised me I should be happy—and how unhappy I was—or wasn't I—I for: get, for now I only see that it's true—and I am happy."

But to her, happiness was not what the many happy people of this earth take to be the only possible happiness—hers was a spiritual state of being which she acquired and kept for years—the sole condition was:

"Come in through one of the doors and sniff the perfume from our altars—the dust of our DIVINE STAGE—and you then shall be happy and be our real servant."

SELDOM has such an easy time been given to anybody as Irving gave to Ellen Terry—all financial responsibility removed . . . for the day that Irving came to engage her, Ellen Terry knew perfectly well that her financial future was safe in his hands. Whether she got sixty pounds or eighty pounds or a hundred pounds a week in London, or two hundred or more in America, I don't know. I have heard of such things: I never saw any reason to concern myself with them when she was alive, and I don't now. I know everybody is tremendously interested in how much everybody else *gets* a week, but I am not. What interests me, as one who cares for the theatre and not what it brings in, is that a permanent state of good can be achieved; and that is what Irving achieved for my mother. For himself as well, of course, and for the rest of the company, for the authors, the designers, the musicians—and for the English theatre most of all.

That is as a sound business man sees—that is to

see and act practically. It is permanency that I have been fighting for, all these years, and I con· sider it a more practical and business·like state for any organization than the condition to which the hectic gamblers of to·day have brought the stage.

Gambling in theatrical work is harmful to every· one in the theatre: experiment is excellent. The difference between experimenting and gambling is this—that the experimenter wants to see how a thing is coming out, in due time; the gambler wants to see how much money is coming out of the thing in two weeks. His logic ceases to be logic, his reason is inane, his commonsense is nonsense: he is con· cerned with but one thought—will this show bring in such and such, and will it bring it in quickly? —if not, it is not practical. The tendency is a mad one: sane men will not gamble with the arts or the sciences.

Now Ellen Terry was particularly sane in this way. The week that she accepted Irving's engage· ment, she had refused one from Augustus Harris of Drury Lane Theatre, because, "Augustus Harris," she said, putting her nose in the air and sniffing, as a keen·scented dog does—"Augustus Harris is not hunting the bird permanency: he is sky·larking with a gamble—and I'm not gambling."

E. T. loved permanency in her work—strange, and yet not so strange, that in life this same permanency had less meaning for her.

But I am tempted to feel that Nelly Terry, in giving up life for a _fixed life-work_ at the Lyceum Theatre with Irving, gave up a thousand times more than she got; and I think there is a certain restlessness in her letters to Bernard Shaw, recently published, which reveals this.

Suppose she had stayed on at Harpenden while she helped to put things straight with those bailiffs. . . . . .

E. T. AND MARRIAGE

I

NELLY had no theories—Ellen Terry had a few. For the institution of marriage she had some understanding, a great respect, but no liking. She married three times, so that it could not be said that she had been unfair to marriage. She gave it a very good chance, and proved it a farce each time—not a unique conclusion to arrive at, but so it was.

But she knew that it was she who was the chief figure in that farce—the comic sad figure around whom all goes badly—always in trouble—always muddling.

First she was married to Mr. G. F. Watts, secondly she married Mr. Charles Kelly, thirdly, Mr. James Carew.

Why was it ever a farce—why did it always end lamentably ? Her husbands were not to blame—it was she who was not a marriageable person—because she was too passionately the servant of the stage . . . no other thing but the stage could absorb her—nothing else could persuade her—she listened only to the counsel it gave her—it was her touchstone—her Bible—her cross and her wings.

If a wonderful person came onto her stage, she loved that person—if a more wonderful, she would love that one more: and while Shakespeare never came near in person, she loved him possibly most of all.

She was always a good deal at the mercy of her imagination—it was a strange state she was in. Here comes Ellen Terry, out of her house, and down the steps, talking to a servant and to a child or two. Getting into a carriage, the great Ellen Terry drives off to a rehearsal at the theatre— stops in Piccadilly and buys some fruit—is hailed by someone in Arlington Street and someone near the Garrick—sees them—calls them by name—kisses them, talks, says yes, says no—but actually Nelly Terry is not seeing, kissing, talking; she is speeding on to the Theatre, and has arrived ahead of the great Ellen Terry.

Once in the place and at work, she has forgotten who the dickens it was she met near the Garrick Club, spoke to in Arlington Street: and out comes a pencil, and she does as she had taught herself to do—writes down the name: " Mr. Bore," or " dear Mrs. Gor‿ don "—prompt copies are covered with such names.

Then, later, she keeps a book, and as she drives along in her carriage one day, down goes a name, "Mr. Wardell:" . . . maybe she writes against this name—"stands erect and looks straight"; why does she write it? only lest she should forget who the deuce it was, this Mr. Wardell.

No one must suppose that she didn't take pains to remember people—she did—but unless they impressed her very powerfully, they just vanished from her memory.[1]

But the name "Irving" she never had need to write down—though she wrote almost daily *to* him

[1] Mr. Graham Robertson writes to me about this :—"One thing strikes me in reading her letters and looking back—that *people* had less influence in her life than might be imagined. Things, thoughts, dreams, memories seemed to affect her more. She would write often and lovingly of her friends with that playful affection that was especially her own, but the note of deep feeling is absent with which she would write or speak of things that really moved her.

"She once wrote to me—*One's work is the best of us all—don't you think so? With most folks I've met, I've loved their work better than them.*

"Though ever now and again in her letters would come a little litany of names that were dear to her. They varied very slightly and might, I think, easily have been cut down to three* which never failed to turn up.

"Here is a long-ago specimen written on an American tour. (About 1907) :

"*Do you love me very much now I am very far away from you? I do you—' and twenty such! '—only—only there aren't twenty. I'm thinking about you—and your mother—and Edward (and Edward)—and Henry—and Ted and Edy—and the work—and the moon—and I just love all and every and can't help it.*

"And I enclose a scrap from a much later letter where you will find the same list—with inconspicuous additions such as Wordsworth and Jimmy Whistler. (*Reproduced opposite page* 166.)

"I am very proud of being included in this litany but am well aware that my appearance is due to the fact that the letters were written to me—and your mother was invariably polite."

* i.e., "Edward, Edy, and Ted."

—she had no need to remind herself that this was the man, the figure-head and very head of the whole house—the whole realm of the Theatre—her world.

HOW could anyone in his kind senses ask such a dear madwoman in marriage—really, a joke's a joke. How could anyone out of the Theatre write a solemn letter to such a sweet mad lady as this? And in the Theatre, how could any actor suppose she was marriageable? Is it customary to marry visions—to espouse harmonies—to be tied to Fairy Queens?

Sensible men never do that, nor do sensible women either—and this book is of course only for these two.

To marry, you go carefully about the business —though some of us, I must admit, marry at twenty-one, divorce at twenty-five, and pay heavily afterwards, year by year, for what can only be described as " a youthful indiscretion." Men who do this act like fools—that is what the law considers them, and very rightly punishes folly. Women, apparently, are never fools in the eyes of the law, however they act, and get seldom punished: men even *allow* themselves to be divorced—men who, by uttering two words, could have divorced their wives. Such idiots deserve to be dubbed " idealists."

I suppose E. T. was impossible as a wife. Great actresses and singers as a rule don't marry with success. Great actresses evidently *must* be impossible people. Bernhardt, Duse, Rachel, Siddons, Jordan, Sophie Arnould, la Gabrielli—I could add a hundred to this brief count of those who were not possible persons as wives.

There is no other explanation for it, and it had best be faced. One can't be possible *every* way . . . I don't see how you can rock the cradle, rule the world, *and* play *Ophelia* perfectly, all in the day's work. The great ladies who want to play-act or sing or dance, are generally obliged to make money. After ten years' hard labour, they manage to make a little. But if it had included being a good, nice, sensible wife, and staying at home and being happy with a sensible man, who is so sensible that he leaves home and goes to his work at 8.30 and returns at 6.30—then it could never have happened.

Of course exceptions occur—Ristori, and possibly another, Isabella Andreini . . . both Italian, by the way. Each of these women was a Roman Catholic, had a family, married very happily— and both were very famous; Isabella the greatest actress of the seventeenth century, Ristori of the nineteenth.

E

NOW it may seem to some people a far-fetched thing to say, but Nelly Terry was very happily married to the stage. I mean it in the sense that whom God hath joined together, let no man put asunder—and E. T. was joined by God to the stage, even as Duse and Bernhardt were. So that if she did a wrong thing, it was not to cleave even more ardently to the stage, it was to attempt marriage at the same time.

It almost seems as though the stage stood in need of a special provision in regard to the law governing marriage—for really, far too many marriages of stage people are failures. Someone, without thinking, will offer this solution of the problem—he will point to the priesthood, and tell us that if the actor is called to the stage by God, as the priest is to the Church, then the actor should abstain from all worldly associations, and remain celibate. There are already some advancing minds in the European Theatre who hold to this theory. Personally, I hold with quite the other view, which would see actors return to some blessed state of distinguished vagabondage from which, alas, a law in the time of Queen Elizabeth rescued the rogues.

But of course, you say—and you wonder that I write in so old-fashioned a way about such matters

—no one to day, you say, fusses about marriage. But I note that every highly placed functionary of State, Church and everywhere else is duly married, and some, anyhow, hold very strict views about the importance of the marriage tie, and even moderns realize its importance for testamentary reasons. They who strictly abide by its rules can evidently do so more easily than they who break the rules . . . but because they are broken is no argument that it is either right or difficult to break them. Let new and better laws and rules be made, by all means (and quickly, too) but till they exist we have to follow those in usage. Exactly—if we can: if we cannot and do not, we and not the rules are at fault. It's as plain as a pikestaff—and I know that Ellen Terry, if she broke any of the rules, did so with regret—never truculently.

She was not an intellectual—she wasn't a dry thinker—she never thought out love, or brought intellect to bear upon a kiss. She never used her matrimonial failures to publicity ends, as prominent women have done before and after her. Of course—of course she shrank from that sort of thing, and if anything, this made her, later on in life, lean towards beguiling the world that she was "respectable" . . . and yet she was so utterly paradoxical that she never ceased from confiding in those she trusted, all about herself.

She trusted rather too many. Among her best friends, those who are now dead were Tom Taylor and Alice Carr, Mrs. Ward Beecher and Mrs. Gillespie and Mrs. Dexter, of America.

But she has many true friends still living. Whenever I have talked with these about her, they have always reminded me of some happening which now makes them laugh and laugh again . . . only her enemies have lingered to tell me that she ever grieved. It was to E. T. rather a sin to grieve.

People always become younger remembering her: just as when living she gave out such buoyancy to support others, so, now she is dead, the help is still there and somehow comes back to those who remember her well.

II

OF my mother's husbands I can record but little —the first, Mr. Watts, I never saw—the second, Mr. Charles Kelly, I remember slightly, but I was about four years old when he came into our family, six when he left; so I retain but a fleeting impression of something large and heavy-footed, a kind of stranger who, I thought, growled and clumped his way along the passages, whereas Mother had seemed to sing or whisper her way, and had flitted in and out.

So much for an impression of childhood. I must have been one of those ridiculously sensitive children, for at four, had my father been walking up and down the house, the sound of his heavy footfall would, I am sure, have enchanted me.

A stepfather, however excellent a man, unless the mother be most willing, cannot do very much to help bring up the stepchildren—and I suppose my mother objected to Charles Kelly flourishing his hunting-crop at us in the Lord of the Manor style, when we made a beastly noise in the morning.

But Kelly was really as kind a bear as it were possible to find. Once he devoted over an hour to trying to teach me the way to read the clock. It was at Longridge Road, and the clock hung in the hall, at the foot of the stairs . . . and spite of my fear over the difficulty of learning anything at all from anybody who began to teach it to me, I did manage, sitting on those stairs, to learn the clock from him.

So I shall always regret that E. T. did not allow him a longer time, if only to teach me some more of the things I should have been glad to learn from him.

As it was, when he vanished, I fell once more into the hands of a house of women—who, lovely as women are, are utterly unsuited to be of the very service they would most like to render.

No one is less suited than a busy actress to cope with her children properly. I recall the attempt made by this dear Mother, just twenty minutes before she had to be off to the Theatre, to teach me how to cheer up and remember a word which stuck in my throat—the last word of a lyric by William Blake. She tells the story in her memoirs.

The verses begin: "*When the voices of children are heard on the green,*" and end up: "*And the hills are all covered with sheep.*"

I could not say "sheep."

I remember this: I saw a looking‹glass—I saw my mama—I saw a window—a wash‹hand‹stand—a sister—a door—a staircase. I saw the way out of the room, but not out of this difficulty, which was, how to make Mama less worried about nothing—i.e., about myself. Neither could I see the reason that impelled all this accuracy of detail . . . why sheep—why not grass—trees—? Dio mio!

The thing ended for me in terror, and she and I were in tears, she says.

Charlie Kelly's tuition ended in success, and without tears.

She supposed that I was being obstinate: *"Nothing* would make him say 'sheep,'" she writes in 1908.

I was put in the corner.

Then it appears my kind little sister, trying to help me, made matters worse. She whispered " sheep " to me.

Any other profiteer would have seized on this and romped away with it—but then it was that I realized that there was something quite wrong in this female way of setting about things. What the deuce does a man, even if only three feet high and about five years old, want with words put into his own mouth, by which he may immediately convict himself of being precisely what the judge and jury thought him—obstinate ? Rather be a plain terrified fool, any day, than an obstinate ass.

Evidently E. T. had no time to remember that —she was due at the Theatre.

I could not think of the one word, " sheep," because I had lost the damn brutes: and E. T. seems to have forgotten, in the hurry of the moment, the whole of another poem by the same old Blake, which runs:

> " But to go to school in a summer morn,
>   O ! it drives all joy away;
>   Under a cruel eye outworn
>   The little ones spend the day
>   In sighing and dismay."

And to a child in a panic, the kindest eyes seem
cruel. A spanking—an unreasonable but season,
able waking-up—is better than a tussle of the
" will " with Mama. I, too, have thought children
obstinate when they were merely panicked—so it
is, and so it will be till the education of children is
left entirely to men and women who have made
a careful study of the whole subject, and who have
been trained to teach.

But for all I may say, I was like most boys of four,
and at the time preferred the petting hands of
women, who I could see at a glance were only putting
on sternness, to those of Kelly—for though kindly,
he was, of course, stern and big: but his appearance
and manner braced one up, whereas theirs relaxed
one. One felt one could sooner or later take advan,
tage of all their soft and killing kindness, but not
of his.

Well, good-bye, Charlie Kelly.

OF my mother's third husband, James Carew, I
could write at length, for a jollier, better
fellow I do not know: but I will reserve that for
my own memoirs—this is a book on Ellen Terry.

My mother married Carew, who is four years my
junior, in 1907. On hearing the news, I felt delighted

that our mother should have the pluck to face that daunting phase of life once more, and I wished her very, very well on her new course; but my sister was, I remember, utterly distraught. She seems to have thought that others have a say in these matters: she was inexperienced and, I think, ignorant of most things to do with life as it is— and somehow or other, prejudiced in some odd way against the male sex, though always kind to me.

I shall ever remember one day in 1878, at Longridge Road, she asked me if I would like to see a portrait of my father—whom I had not seen since I was three years old and could not remember— and instantly she whipped out a terrible drawing someone had made for her, of a fiend with long teeth and claws and a tail, and said: " There—that's him ! " That was meant as kind.

It reminds me a little of a story about Henry Irving. His two sons were looking at a photograph of him, and a lady asked them, " Do you know who that is ? " " Yes," they cried, with joy, " it's Father." " No," said she, " it is a Baboon."

Well, that sort of delusion is too sad, and won't do. It may be true that the male is a demon and a baboon—all I know is that it is not possible for another human being to take up such a lofty and intolerant attitude towards anyone or anything. It does remind us forcibly of Maule's appeal to the court—the famous: " My Lords—we are vertebrate animals, we are mammalia! my learned friend's manner would be intolerable in Almighty God to a black beetle."

The custom—the attitude—may be universal; I hope it is not—but it's uncanny and horrible. It is not the fault of the lady, perhaps—certainly could not be the fault of my sister, who at eight or nine years old could not have achieved infallibility, nor have failed to feel that old love which we do bear towards our fathers as well as our mothers—whoever we are.

No, the fault here does not lie with my sister— it cannot. Some damn female nurse, or someone, had been poisoning her mind, perhaps, through their thoughtless chatter.

So when she grew up, and came to the experience of seeing my mother married to James Carew, my sister disapproved. Now my mother had, to my knowledge, never disapproved of what we did, thought, felt or said. Always kindness and always excuses for us.

Having seen life, and known what it was to be now and again in the wrong, and even to do wrong, she never posed as infallible, nor could she ever fail to find in her heart forgiveness for anyone's acts: even the unco' guid she could forgive. She was ever quick to help as well as sympathise with us all.

How possibly be out of sympathy with her, when, for once, she did as she wished, without stopping for silly approvals or disapprovals?

NELLY AND E. T. QUARREL

AND BRING UP THE CHILDREN

A Dialogue—
Harpenden

(*E. T. left standing in the road, looking at Charles Reade as he rides away, his coat-tails flapping up and down.*)

NELLY TERRY: What on earth do you think you are doing?

Ellen Terry: Mind your own business—I have made up my mind.

Nelly Terry: I don't think you've got a mind worth making up.

Ellen Terry: The playing of Shakespeare improves a woman's mind far more than washing a couple of brats.

Nelly Terry: Yes—if you look on them as brats. I have two children——

Ellen Terry: They aren't yours—they're mine.

Nelly Terry: You take one, I'll keep the other.

Ellen Terry: Yes, we will toss up !

Nelly Terry: No, we won't. You've got such grand ideas of what women should be, suppose you experiment on the girl.

(*Here Nelly dropped three tears.*)

Ellen Terry: Done ! (*In imitation of Charles Reade.*)

E. T. was always getting in the way of my mother . . . I continue to speak of them as two, because although one and the same person, they were leagues apart and agreed to differ on almost every subject—especially on that subject so important to all women, the rearing of children.

E. T. had "ideas" and "theories" about that, whereas Mother had none, or rather, but one—the everlasting and old-fashioned idea consisting of acts: getting up early, waking the children gently—getting them up—washing and dressing them—then seating them round a table and giving them their bread-and-milk, which she had prepared carefully long before—in some instances going still earlier to fetch the milk and the bread from the dairy and the baker's.

Our mother's sole idea, when we were quite young, went on just so, right through the day.

Hourly care of her two children, and when not *with* them for a few hours or moments during the day, then she would be preparing things for them —food—clothes—washings—cleanings—twenty to thirty things, doing most of it herself. Meantime, be it understood, she had to see to household affairs; that means perhaps another ten things to be remembered—to be seen to—and done well. All these things to be done were included in Mother's one idea of how to bring up the children she had borne. She had had experience very early in life, and not only had seen her own mother feeding, washing, brushing, mending and what not for her younger sisters and brothers, but had, when called on, lent a hand.

She had, just as early, an experience in acting —do not forget this: and E. T. and our mother— two people in one—went on growing side by side . . . not at war—not at peace—but in a state of armed neutrality.

Before long my mother, Nelly, gave to E. T. the bringingup of my sister—and then it was that E. T. came out with all her "theories." She told my mother that she'd soon show her what a grand result could be achieved with the daughter, and left her to deal with the son.

E. T. was the " strongest " of the two, but Mother was more cunning, and the dearest—no woman could possibly have been a better mother, a truer wife, a more faithful, un-swerving guardian and guide to a house than she, had it not been for E. T.—that public person who came between us.

It was in these terms she thought of herself, and once told me so. It was a wonderful talk—almost a monologue—in which she laid bare the truth about the life of the actress.

We were sitting in the dining-room at 215 King's Road, Chelsea—the last house she loved—an old seventeenth or eighteenth century house, full of the few things she had cared to collect—the chairs, tables, bookshelves and sideboard designed for her by my father, and books, pictures and china: and there one evening she sat and talked, just as a mother now and again will do with a son.

Of people and of hopes and doubts—not *much* about the doubts . . . but when she came to speak of herself, she asked me if I thought she had been a good mother. When I said, " A glorious one," she made a motion of the hands, and " No, no—no," she said. And then and there went on to tell me that she knew what a mother was—" Elena is the perfect mother . . . *all* the time for you and for Teddy and Nellie[1]—*all* the time—all the time. Quiet, steady, true. No horrible 'theatre'—no public life apart from and parting from the dear private life of love to you three—none."

" I so imperfect," she went on, " unable to be one thing or another . . . never *entirely* one, never *entirely* the other " (as she wrote, so she talked, with plenty of underlinings or italics).

She sat there, telling me what had been for more than thirty years in her mind to tell me, of her shortcomings—never once making any excuses for failures, or saying anything foolish or weak, but calmly reviewing the past.

Nothing had been too " difficult " for her—that was not a word she would ever make use of—only, " but I was such a fool—such a *fool* "; that was my mother speaking . . . more than that, she was rending E. T. from head to foot—no armed neutrality then—attack, and a merciless one.

I loved and adored this Mother—the dear little thing—and once and again I saw her as I saw her that evening—and she would dress up and do things and say things to conjure back the impression which she knew I loved to receive—that she was really, all said and done, only Mother, and no less. For if

[1] My children.

others were blind to this delicate sensitive truth, she was not—and she knew how a son, and perhaps only a son, can feel and think about it all. She knew I often came to the house to find her, and found her flown, and E. T. seated in her place . . . a mother-in-art—which is only one remove from a mother-in-law.

It is not easy for any son to find any pleasure in seeing his mother being slowly transformed into a public person.

When a dear mother has to be at the same time a very celebrated public person, it cannot be too easy for her. For the mother, whether she be a Queen, an actress or a doctor, is the same thing—all-important— more than all else: and whatever public office is thrust upon her, she remains the human being.

TAKE, for example, the mother of the young man Louis XIV—the venerable Queen-Mother Anne of Austria.

What a mother ! . . . and what an extraordinary woman—and in what a difficult situation she is placed, having to be a mother and a Queen at the same time.

There are caricatures of the time showing that highly respected and much loved First Gentleman of Europe, as a lad, standing in the corner of the

F

room, to which his mother has sent him. You
hear of him arriving rather late at the Palais Royal,
and his mother's eyes resting on him, and he per-
spiring as if he had been running six miles.

Consider the fond mind of this dear Queen Anne
of Austria, and let us listen to its workings.

Surrounded by the Court, Louis appears, skulking
behind a pillar—in riding breeches. He is wiping
his nose with a blue cotton handkerchief which the
gamekeeper at Fontainebleau has given him. He is
now stuffing it in an ungainly way into his breeches
pocket. The Court, eyes turned on the Queen-
Mother, can see him with its sidelong glance.

What is she to say, this dear mother—what is
she to look? She wants to say: "Yes, Louis dear,
I hope you have enjoyed yourself. Did you kiss
the gamekeeper's daughter? And do take your
boots off, that I may see if your socks are wet. Why
isn't Jeannette there to look after you?"

And as these phrases rapidly shimmer up from
the mother's heart, the Queen almost faints—she
sees the whole Court—the whole world—looking at
her.

Then it is that she tightens up, tighter than the
Court, and anathematises that thing which calls
itself the future King of France. One look is enough
—one look of love and agony, which the Prince,

like all fond sons, hasn't even the wit to translate correctly. All he can murmur to himself (in French) is, " Going to get it hot in half an hour ! "

And it is true, he does get it hot—not because there is any love lacking, only because he had punished her, through the Court, so unmercifully— the reaction has been too great for her.

IN E. T.'s case there was no Court, but there was always the public—E. T. was always aware of the public outside: and I think E. T. always looked on me as any fond parent will—that is, as 'twere the Prince of all Princes of the Earth.

Let me try and remember instances in which I found her extremely hard . . .

I have sat thinking for over an hour, and have not been able to remember one.

And then excessively tender. . . . Well, I can hardly recall any moment when she was not exces, sively tender.

With Nelly helping her, she became a perfect mother: and this is all the more extraordinary when you realize one more very important point—that there was no father in the house to share with her the difficulties of bringing up two children—and one of them a boy.

II

MY Mother was born not exactly in poverty
—her father and mother, by their acting
together, made a fair livelihood and provided for
a numerous family: but their income cannot have
been sufficient—for as soon as the first girl, Kate,
was a few years old, she too tucked up her sleeves
and lent a hand at helping things along—she went
to the theatre and worked like a Trojan. It was the
way with the Terrys. And when Ellen, the second
girl, could make a funny face and speak some lines
with some sense, she too toddled off to the theatre
and did her bit.

She never set out to make money—she took to
theatre work quite easily, and realized that so long
as she could work, she could get money.

She seldom bothered anyone—she was bothered
. . . her genius bothered her (that was Ellen Terry);
but she knew one thing, and knew that as well as
she knew her own face. She knew that if she held
fast to her genius and never tinkered with it, never
theorized about things, never allowed anything to
interfere with its development and expression—she
knew that she would succeed—become well off—
be able to pay for herself and us—and bring me up.

ELLEN TERRY
about 1880   (32)

"What do you want to be when you grow up?"
she asked me—and I replied, "A clown or a cab-
driver." That was when I was six or seven.

It was difficult for her—difficult to know exactly
what education a really good cab-driver would
require . . . as for a clown, perish the thought—
"'An actor,' he means." But I meant no such
thing—I meant nothing: I assure you that my mother
had been so terribly kind to me in my first ten to
fifteen years of existence, that by the time I was
eighteen I was as helpless as a penny toy in a shop
window.

The blessed lady, my mother, no more knew how
to bring up a boy than she knew how to swim—
and by the way, once we were both nearly
drowned together in shallow water at Boulogne
when I was about five years old. She could have
brought up my little sister Edy—but she wouldn't—
she was too frightened of making a mistake and
being told later by her, "I told you you didn't
do it right." So she ever flattered that bit of
goods, and spoiled *this* bit.

Edy was "wonderful"—poor old Edy: she had
but to frown and say "Won't" for the greatest
actress of the age to cry "marvellous!" and "hush!"
to everyone, and repeat, "isn't she really marvellous!"

And the son, what of him?—when I consider my mother, I have nothing good to say for the son.

Until I found friends to begin to help me as I wanted to be helped, I count my development as nil. I was born sleepy—fat, fair-haired and fast asleep . . . a gourmand—a sensualist—a conceited lump—and a dreamer.

Not all pleasant dreams . . . I dreamed awful dreams when I was about six years old. I would wake in the middle of the night, terrified by I know not what kind of dream—for it consisted in my being in a crushing mill and out of it and watching— going into it—drawn screaming in and up into it and through it—and no hope of escape. I would wake and cry and be unable to stop—and someone —once my mother—would come in and say it was all right; and still, though awake, I was terrified and cried because it was so awful. What was awful?—I cannot say more than I have said—it was the dream, the immense and irresistible horror of something going round and round and about to crush me.

E. T. was acting *Ophelia* or *Lydia Languish,* and so I suppose I was allowed to eat a pork pie— maybe it was that. Yet I am sure careful instruc- tions were given to the many women who were in the house to put me early to bed, and give me only bread and butter and warm milk for supper. Then perhaps it was something else—some forma* tion of the skull or brain—or . . . could it have been that I inherited a vivid imagination—an imagination which was affected by any shadow seen in a room—any far*off recollection of some cry heard years before—or some machine spoken of?

I have often wondered why I suffered so much in that way—and suffer I did.

Added to which, I was a coward. I was afraid of the dark, and afraid of certain pictures. There was one picture of a cat, with big immovable eyes, sitting crouched up in a hole, looking at me—I used to shudder on seeing it, and cry out " Pussy in the dark ! " . . . I remember it now. The awful thing was that it was accompanied by music, and two candles lit, which occasionally quivered.

E. T., when she had a free evening, would play to us on the piano. She had a book of short songs, and to each song was a picture. On page 9 was the Cat—the terror.

She would begin with one song about " Little Bo*Peep," maybe, and pass on to " Jack Horner " —already I was in a state of terror. Standing on one side of the upright cottage piano—my sister on the other—I watched the pages turn over, steadily and slowly, and waited for the horror that was coming—it must come, I knew.

First song done, second song over, third song . . . fifth . . . eighth . . . and now for the ninth—a turn, and lo, there it is—the ghastly " Pussy in the dark ! "

I do not know what happened—whether I was told not to be so silly—but I know that this terrible picture on page 9 put a greater fear into me than I ever received before or after. The terror that is in those stories, *The Turn of the Screw*, by Henry James, or *The Mystery of the Rue Morgue*, by Poe, is nothing to it. I was wet with fear, and it haunted me for months—and maybe longer. There is no doubt that I was a great coward when my imagination came to be played upon—though in the way of adventures, in fights at school and in football, I did not shirk. It was the dark, and all that accompanies the fading of the light, that I could not stand.

IN her memoirs, E. T. tells how we were brought up on Walter Crane books—but I remember that Caldecott and George du Maurier played a big part in our picture life—and Blake's pictures. And we often went for hideously long walks all over London—I think a three-hour walk was not unusual. Unfortunately, E. T. couldn't spare mother Nelly to go with us, so the walk was never what it might have been. E. T. was always separating us from Nelly.

Sometimes I remember seeing her down at Hampton Court, where we had a cottage—Rose Cottage, it was called. It looked out on the Bushey Park, which —unlike the Rooky wood—was gay with fat round trees—chestnuts—and here and there a May-tree— and stags and does . . . from the back windows we could see the stags fighting—and we would search for the antlers which came off.

We would also eat lots of ices, which were made at a shop close by, which I believe is still flourishing —and drink ginger-beer at the gates to the Palace gardens—and see Mother whenever she came down from London.

I was never tired of going through the rooms of the Palace. There were pictures, many more than one could see in most places—Henry VIII and Francis I meeting on the Field of the Cloth of Gold—Henry had his head cut out, I believe, and a new one was put in—one saw the circular mark clearly—I saw it again only the other day. And the fine ladies painted by Sir Peter Lely—and the silver chandelier—and the immense four-poster beds with slim, towering posts wrapped in damask, and curtains falling from high up, and a bunch of plumes at each top corner. Wonderful beds!

But more lovely than all these, to me, was the warm, cool air which came in through the open windows—twenty, thirty, forty tall windows—and the glimpses of trees and lawns, and the sound of the fountains playing outside.

Meantime, what of Ellen Terry, what of Nelly? I have been searching for them in remembrance, and cannot find either—both were busy rehearsing and acting, when we were busy feeding the gold-fish.

I am sure that it is much more important to feed goldfish than to perform in a theatre—but if you are a child, I suppose it is more enjoyable to do so with your mother and father than with some stranger; and if you can't have both, one will do.

At Hampton Court, it was very enjoyable.

E. T. AND OUR MOTHER JOIN FORCES

I

WHEN I was sixteen years old, my mother determined that I should go upon the stage and become an actor: so I was given the name Edward Henry Gordon Craig, and then and there I was christened as such—for it seems that when an infant this christening ceremony had been forgotten by my parents. Lady Gordon and Henry Irving were my godmother and godfather—everyone seemed most cheerful, and I felt uncommonly depressed. Why any church ceremonial should be depressing to the young, I do not know, but it has that effect quite often.

In the same year 1888 my mother sent my sister to Berlin to study music. She lived with a musician and his wife, and learnt to play the piano very well.

In 1889 I was put on the stage.

If you are to take to the stage as a duckling takes to water, you must be put to it young—seventeen is too old. Six years old is about the right age if you are to take to it and absorb it quite easily. If at six years old, when I walked onto the stage of the Court Theatre, I had been kept there, I should have swum without study, without being conscious that I was swimming, and by seventeen would have been an able craftsman. Whereas at seventeen I was disas٫ trously self٫conscious. I was not exactly a stick, and I could do better than some—but after all, what is that ? By the age of seventeen one should have acquired much experience. I had none—and I had received no tuition. Experience *or* tuition is necessary.

The Lyceum Theatre, in 1889 when I first stepped onto its boards, had no training school—and I was given a part straight away, and five pounds a week for playing it. "*What* a chance," cried the thoughtless— " What a wonderful opportunity—lucky young dog!"

I was always being overwhelmed by enthusiastic people who shook me, poked me, clapped me on the back, depressed me, irritated and exhausted me, by asking, first if I did not appreciate what a great privilege it was to be working with such great artists as H. I. and E. T., and then, how I liked it ?

Naturally one likes to do well—to feel one is being of use and to work under the eye of Irving, and to have E. T. there—were the people utter idiots who pestered me with such questions, badgering me for answers where there were no answers ?

I had been on the stage before—in "Olivia," when I was about six years old, I had walked on among the supers—and in Chicago in 1885 I had played the small part of a gardener's boy in "Eugene Aram." Why the dickens I was not kept to the stage from that time onwards, if it was an *actor* they wanted, it is difficult to discover. But it was all in the hands of E. T., who took the advice of first one friend, then another, with the result that it was decided to send me to school—to give me that unnecessary thing, a bit of education. For actors need not be sent to schools and colleges. Education, valuable to most men, is, more often than not, quite fatal to an actor, the one thing to preserve being the child in him. Some people even hold that it would be best if he could not read—an exaggerated theory which we need not go into here.

A T the Lyceum Theatre I was pointed out as Ellen Terry's son, which for a beginner was rather an ordeal, and of the wrong kind. To work unnoticed was all I wanted to do, and, to be lost among the others—to take my time —to pick up the right idea by walking on—and to emerge in time as a good actor. To-day the idea "slow and sure" may be of no use at all in those walks of life where the motor, electricity, wire‹ less and the rest have ordered the pace to be " full speed ahead." But in theatrical work there is no need for this " full speed ahead "—if not an art, it is some‹ thing of the same nature as music, painting, architec‹ ture, and speed has very little to do with the arts.

People nowadays skip the preparation necessary to every craft, and even declare that preparation is quite unnecessary. If you assert that eighteen months is not too much time to train a man to speak and walk properly, unless he has begun at a very early age, men who are excessively careful over their own work, and who will never hurry it, will write to the papers to say that six weeks is quite long enough for a mere actor.

Ellen Terry was trained for fully three years before she learnt how to speak properly. Mrs. Charles Kean taught her to some extent, with the rest of the troupe, at rehearsals:

" 'A, E, I, O, U, my dear,' she used to say, ' are five distinct vowels, so don't mix them up all together as if you were making a pudding. If you want to say *I am going on the river*, say it plainly, and don't tell us you are going on the *rivah !* You must say *her*, not *har;* it's *God*, not *Gud :* remonstrance, not remun‹ strance,' and so forth."

And so when, in 1889, rehearsals began for " The Dead Heart," my mother helped me at these rehearsals

—especially in the two scenes which I had to play with her. At a rehearsal she had a way of making all things easy . . . difficulties vanished as she showed you what to do and how you might do it; and she always rendered you comfortable.

"You do *so*—yes, that's it—and *so*—now over here—and there we are."

A thing was not good to her (after her seven years' training and two years' apprenticeship) if it could not be done easily. When a whole part went easily with her, it was superlatively good work she gave us—it was the swan swimming.

As she breathed, so she rehearsed—all she expressed was expressed so—and she could show you how to do anything you might ask her, if she was actually standing on the stage at the time, and at work on a play she had studied. It was rather different if you were not on a stage at the time, for the boards were an essential to her. If, without notice, you asked her in the house what to do in such and such a part, then she might be suddenly at sea. "You begin—the rest follows" seems to have been all the theory she indulged in: just as, if asked "how does one breathe?" that would be the answer— "You begin—first one breath, then another."

Which is very right and good for the born actor, who goes onto the stage at six years old, and gets seven or eight years' training there: and this would seem to prove that as a rule none but born actors should drift onto the stage. To-day we find all sorts of people there, but far too seldom an actor —and very rarely a fine artiste.

MY mother was evidently ambitious for me to become a good actor and a successful one: and it was in 1889, when I began, that she and E.T. made up their quarrel and agreed to join forces. It was settled between them that I was to become a good actor; but how this was to be accomplished was not decided—for there was no master at that time to give the necessary training. Admiration such as some of us young actors had for Irving, did not train—it exhausted us. At the best, all it led to was an imitation of his peculiarities.

The Lyceum Theatre was my only " school." Experience teaches you something, but it seldom develops your discernment. That is what a good master, with sufficient time, can do. He can show you the several ways of acting—he can always point out the way he believes best adapted to your own capacities, and say why—he will not over-strain you, nor let you think too little of yourself—and without urging you to any excess of originality, he can always help you to avoid being too tame. If you have a little talent, he can do something towards increasing it—if you have much talent, he can prevent you from squandering it. Good masters and good theatre schools are to be found to day in most of the capitals of Europe.

E.T. obtained masters for me for fencing, for drilling, and for French. A very cele brated man tried to teach me French: once or twice a week he came to Barkston Gardens and sat for an hour reading Molière with me. He was, I believe, a proper sort of master, but I was assuredly a dunce of a pupil: and as, owing to my own stupidity, I know French still very imperfectly to this day, I won't dishonour him by naming him.

I was taught fencing at an Academy owned by Jem Mace; and drilled at the Knightsbridge Barracks —three times a week, I think.

This shows how active E.T. was to get me masters of French, fencing and deportment—but after all, some tuition in acting was what I needed.

So I attended for a few weeks at the hotel where Mr. Walter Lacy—a very old man then—sat in state from ten till eleven, in the dusky front parlour —one of the smallest I ever saw.

There, for three quarters of an hour, I sat at a table and bawled or piped blank verse at Mr. Walter

G

Lacy; and he, to give me some idea how not to bawl or pipe, would, where he saw an opening, stop me and relate a theatrical anecdote illustrative of something or other, but of what was never clear . . . it would be, in any case, very pleasant, for it made me laugh, and Mr. Lacy would at once join in—and together we would rock to and fro on our two chairs, in the dusky morning in the small room in the Portland Hotel: I think that was its name.

I liked these visits to Mr. Lacy—they left me with the confident feeling that acting possessed no difficulties, for we sat and read, and there an end. I cannot imagine that Mr. Lacy could have written encouraging my mother to any great extent—he probably wrote to the effect that the best thing she could do in the circumstances would be to put me in a travelling company, with lots of work to do. If so, she took no notice of this suggestion, for I continued at the Lyceum for another seven years.

EVERY evening we would drive down to the Theatre in a carriage with one horse; and when there were rehearsals, I would often drive down to these with her. Occasionally during the drive there would be a word said about the work we were going down to—but not often. We drove along the full length of the Cromwell Road, a street at no time conducive to conversation—but on issuing out again into the light of day, into the bright bustle of Brompton, the pulse did quicken to some extent, and we would turn to our parts and study them.

At the calf age, study is not too serious; so that all I did was to learn the words. What I should have done was to learn the world. But schoolmasters, tutors, mothers and aunts are one and all for teaching you anything they *don't* know, rather than allow the young pupil to learn the one and only valuable thing—the world. Only a man can teach you that by showing it to you, and until I was well past twenty-one I never came across anyone who thought the world was a proper place to know: one was expected to pass it by—to hurry through it—to hope for the best and to forgive it all its sins, without quite knowing their names.

In this mood I would descend the steps of Barkston Gardens and enter the landau with the one horse, and E.T. would put her feet up—a thing called "sticks" having been fixed between the front and back seat for her, so as to rest her properly.

It was pleasant, of course, to sit next to E.T. and see the shops go by, but this was sometimes spoilt for me, because E.T. would stop at a house in the Cromwell Road and call for Miss Audrey Campbell—a young lady of peach-like appearance and a fluttering way, for whom, after a few years, I managed to awaken a dormant jealousy. I wanted my mother all to myself, and the presence of this young lady was one of the first threats of a serious rift. " Perish the thought " served well enough for a few years, but after that, there is no doubt at all about it, I felt a bit jealous.

It was the carriage that did it. There one was with E.T. in a magic boat for two—horse and coachman looking eagerly forward—and plenty of adventures, like passing DEAR ROBERT HEATH, arriving at the Wellington Monument, and gliding down along the Green Park—having Giuliano's pointed out to one—then a glimpse of Solomons, the fruiterer, with its window dressed with stupendous figs, peaches, pears, and the rarest of pineapples— a window full of colour and expensiveness. Then the Burlington Arcade—Sotheran's—and the last pause of the traffic at Piccadilly Circus.

In those days a pause in the traffic was a rare occurrence; vehicles travelled along not very quickly, but generally arrived in time. Two or three stops from Barkston Gardens to the Lyceum Theatre would be the most one would encounter—all the rest of the time the little horses drew their cabs,

broughams, victorias and landaus at a gentle pace—
very reliable, and delightful too, for many reasons.

Never a horn would we hear hooted, from one
end of London to the other, unless it was that of the
coach setting out from Hatchett's Hotel—and that
horn was tootled, not hooted, and never rasped or
squeaked.

It was a delicious drive with mother down to the
Lyceum; it was a bit drowsy and altogether lulled
one into a dream.

The last part of the drive took us down the
Strand, and we turned up Burleigh Street, stopping
at the first door on the right—I think it was the first
door.

This was the private entrance to the Theatre—
not the Stage Door, which was in that day further
up and round the corner, in Exeter Street. This
private entrance in Burleigh Street originally led
through a long and narrow passage to the Royal
Box on the first tier: but as the passage passed by
the rooms which Irving used as his offices, he had
a door made in the wall, and was thus able to reach
his rooms without going by way of the Stage Door.

In connection with this office of H.I.'s, I have a
letter from my Mother, written on October 12th,
1906, in which she says, referring to his death
in 1905:

"To-morrow Henry will have been away a whole year. It only seems to me as if he had left the stage to go into ' the Office ' for an hour (as he so often did at rehearsal) and that it is all rather boring and useless until he comes back."

Everyone else used the general stage door in Exeter Street, but H.I. and E.T. used the private door in Burleigh Street. When I went in with my mother, to carry something for her, I also used this door, but as a rule I would leave her and go round by the door provided for the troops.

There sat Barry, the stage door-keeper, behind a glass-windowed partition, glowering kindlily at all who came in, giving us our letters, and never allowing any but the actual company to pass.

It was a long way from the stage door to the stage, and led through two pairs of swing doors, down a narrow but straight staircase, into one of the scene docks, which in 1799 had been Change Court —now roofed in and become the Lyceum Theatre stage and docks. A glorious place, which vanished when they turned it into a music hall, rebuilding it nearer to the heart's desire of that time—1900 or thereabouts.

Those passages, dark and dangerous, must have seemed awful to any organizing mind which put safety first and play-acting nowhere: and this organizing mind has perfected our passages until hardly a play-actor is left to walk down them.

II

GETTING into the Lyceum by the stage door and down the dark and dreadful passage, I would arrive at the stage, on the prompt side—and would see my mother on the other side—the O.P. side—at which she had arrived by coming along the somewhat less murky passage leading from the private entrance.

We would both find the whole Company assembled in the sun which poured down, even on foggy days, and lit up the clearing in that dark forest which we call the stage. There they were, already assembled —for E.T. could not be punctual, and before long I found I had to get down to the Theatre before her, unless I wanted to be half an hour late. It's strange that the discipline of Mrs. Charles Kean at the Princess's Theatre, which she went through, never taught her punctuality. She *could not* be punctual: Irving could not fail to be.

And on arriving at the sunlit clearing, there one would find him—in the centre of a small group, consisting of Loveday, H. K. Barnett, and other assistants. And lo! Ellen Terry sweeps in—and subsides at once, melting into the whole place— never in any way being "the great E.T." No one was able to melt into a place as she could—which was as well, considering her lack of punctuality.

But this sunlit glade in the forest—this warm stage of rehearsal time. . . . Ravishingly beautiful is the only description—deliciously warm—raggedly tidy—carpeted only by the glorious red boards—those boards on which the feet of Irving and Ellen Terry passed and passed, as they stepped through *Iago* or *Ophelia*, *Shylock* or *Portia*, *Hamlet* and *Dubosc*— *Beatrice*. These boards are gone—how could a nation let them go? Not only sentiment but logic should have preserved them intact.

Above and around these boards hung innumer‹ able cords—some taut, lashed to cleats, others hung loose over our heads, coming we knew not from where . . . we knew vaguely, of course, but we didn't enquire further—we actors don't bother very much what they do up there or down under, or at the side—for the centre of the clearing is ours— let the gnomes, the stage carpenters, scene‹shifters and their masters, burrow and climb and look like elves and monkeys in the forest—we are the Gods of the place. Occasionally one of these furtive creatures would roam from a dark corner into the full glare of the rehearsal sunlight, looking white-faced and worried—but we hardly noted their existence, and never knew their names.

Their chiefs we knew—Arnott, Jimmy, Allen, Fillery and a few more—but, poor brutes, they soon disappeared into the shadows—there, we supposed, to grub for acorns.

AND now this sparkling glade is all astir: our chief, the great Irving, has said, " Very good . . . yes . . . yes . . ." (a light clap of one hand on the other) and—" begin the piece."

And in a moment everyone scatters, and all is once more as still as a deserted glade.

Strange sight—a stage half set; with a rock here —a painted rock, flat, and casting a long, thin shadow on the floor; a couple of cathedral doors leaning against one of the stage walls; by the side of these doors, three pine trees leaning, and in front of them a large gondola, in two pieces, with a big black stove of the eighteenth century close to it, and a man sitting on it, reading his part. Half a street is standing upright towards the centre of the stage, held in place by wooden supports fixed to the stage, and by wire cables attached to ropes going far up into the flies.

And as one turns one's head and looks around, on all sides one sees piled/up pieces, of strange shapes and strangely coloured pattern; boxes with a slit in them—they look like mammoth money/boxes—all standing rigidly eccentric, their inappropriate juxtaposition rendering each piece ridiculous, and yet appearing to us quite natural. We move around among these evidences of an eccentric existence in the most normal way.

SILENCE reigns in the sunlit glade—only the quiet, staccato voice of the Chief, rapping out his orders briefly, and a rapid but rare gesture or two —nothing but this breaks into the dream—the absolute dream—into which the members of the company, robber/band or fanatical crew are now sunk.

The abnormal is the order of the day: the strange has become standardized. We are off.

I hear myself called by name—not by my street name—by the name of the character I am becoming, and which in some fifteen more days I shall have become.

I move towards the voice, and find myself at a fireplace which has no wall, and would to the uninitiated seem sadly out of place. A gnome or two have put it there a few moments earlier, and now I have to go through it, carrying my mother—carrying the great Ellen Terry—in my arms.

It is a tallish fireplace, but I have to stoop—I do stoop, because it is really the mouth of a cave, as I have read in my part.

I stoop with her—how is it she is as light as a child of six—how can I stoop, move on stooping, straighten up—go on, and finally lower her gently to the floor ? It must all be the art of acting, I suppose, for it can't be the art of gymnastics, and I'm not particularly muscular. Yes, it is a scrap of the art of the acting of Ellen Terry—that power of forcing the soul and through the soul, the body . . . for I couldn't have lifted E.T. out of her carriage and carried her in through the solid doorway of the private entrance to the Lyceum; but I can lift and carry her when she calls herself _Imogen,_ and we pass easily through the magic cave and out into the sunlit grove—and I could do it a hundred times and not feel tired. All the art of Ellen Terry.

And now I am speaking—I am aware that I am, because I hear my voice saying the lines:

"Fear no more the frown o' the great,
  Thou art past the tyrant's stroke,"

and my mother is lying on the ground at my feet.

The sun seems to have gone down, and I seem

to be at the edge of the sea—for in front of me is an immense void, except for what seem to be the white caps of breakers, rolling in in a line—and yet they are but the rows of stalls, covered up with their dust cloths.

A CLAP of the hands, and the rehearsal stops. I was just about to pretend to drop one or two imaginary flowers upon Nelly, when the clap of the hands came. Nelly draws herself together and squats like an Indian from Benares, with her back to the Chief, looking up at me and grinning at me all the encouragement of a lifetime.

I catch the ball and toss it back—but quickly attend to business and to the Chief, with sententious calm.

He is asking a question—it is not at first clear to me whether he is addressing the whole glade, my brother Ben, or myself. Ben (called Webster when you got outside the magic circle, and could get hold of a thing called a poster or a programme) ever ready to take the blame the Chief is kind enough to offer gratuitously to the whole circle of braves, asks if he shall stand a little further up stage —no, down stage—" the beetle/crushers "—oh yes . . . he is alluding to our appalling big boots— mine, for Ben's are dandy's.

We are aware that the Chief is moving now—he is going to act. E.T. has now turned her head, because she never missed a moment when H.I. was going to act: and H.I. is just about to show Ben and myself how a young savage should not stand when he is grieving over a dead friend—and H.I. would have done so, but he caught E.T.'s eye looking at him . . . and that immediately has a disastrous effect. Instead of a parody of our poses, he really does something so astoundingly beautiful that no actor on earth or off it could have caught it and gone and done likewise. H.I. was, after all, a sentimentalist. "Try it like that, my boy: something like that . . ." and back he goes to his chair close to the footlights.

We "try it like that," and produce something as unlike that as Primrose Hill is to the Matterhorn. Irving has unfortunately given us one touch of nature plus art which makes the whole theatrical world reel—and no one, not even Talma himself, could have caught the notion.

It was often thus that Irving acted at rehearsals, in that warm, sunlit, magic spot, the Lyceum stage, with the amber lights slightly checked. A few of us were aware how remarkable were his rehearsal per‹ formances of the characters he was not down in the programme to play; but on many they were entirely

lost. I always regret that E.T. was not present at the
night rehearsal when Irving was showing Haviland the
way to play the part of the *Fool* in "King Lear,"
act 2. With, " Let me hire him too—here's my cox⁄
comb," in slithering, far⁄off tones, he feathered onto
the stage—sideways—lopped an imaginary cap, and
floated two steps, till he alighted on the edge of a
table, where he smiled once—and then blew out the
smile.

This passage he repeated, for Haviland's assistance,
several times, several ways, each way as lovely and as
grey as those refrains in an old song, which repeat,
yet have ever something a touch different as they
return.

All the wisdom of philosophy and the learning
of the sages cannot create these moments, and when
he can do it an actor is every whit the equal in
creative power of a fine poet.

We do best when we can recognize these things,
and not cavil because other things are not for the
having. When I was present at these rehearsals or
performances, I saw nothing could be better than
these moments—and in a play, Irving and Ellen
Terry gave us hours of such moments.

When I left this magic place I carried away
remembrances which I treasure still, and shall ever

treasure: without criticising, I have gone my way and attempted to find another path.

How dared that old Sage of Whitehall Court, who was present at the Lyceum, fail to appreciate, since he went there in duty bound, as a critic, to speak the truth ? Is the truth about Bernard Shaw only that which he is not ?—surely it is that which he is—and he is assuredly the most clever, the most adroit, the most widely-listened to journalist who ever lived. I have come to realize that it does not matter a scrap that he is not an artist—never was and never will be. That's his affair: if we cannot appreciate what he is, we lose G.B.S. He could have been very useful to the Government twenty years ago as a publicist, and we took him for a clown—a paradoxical philosopher—a dramatist ! All of which he is not.

"It does not do to take G.B.S. seriously," wrote Ellen Terry—and as we drove home from rehearsal, she would sometimes speak of him, and occasionally of William Archer, whom, I'm grieved to say, she did not take any more seriously than his friend Shaw.

Critics, to actors, are nobodies. Actors do not like blame from a critic, and they do like praise, but they never quite recognize the existence of the critic. He *has* to write—that's what the actor thinks

—and a damn difficult job it must be—but that's all. Just a plague, like mosquitoes or locusts—a plague. But the critics don't think that way at all —they take themselves to be very sorely tried men. The desire to " fling half a brick " springs eternal in the critic's breast: actors never are, but always to be cursed.

A FIRST night performance of a play at the Lyceum Theatre was a thing to have experienced. In front of the curtain all was easy— but behind it—on the stage—all was easier. And the success of each first night is to be attributed to the sureness with which H.I. came down to give battle, and the security with which we all followed him.

In helping towards this, Ellen Terry played a very important part. She exhaled confidence . . . it was not to be talked—things are far too grave for that on a first night—but great personalities can give out so much gay force that it serves to inspire everyone around them—and this she did. The mere sight of her did it.

There are actors and actresses to-day who still do this; but those of us who passed many years at the Lyceum, and were in at a number of first nights, like to believe that never again will there be anything like we experienced with Irving and E.T. leading us.

Were she with me now, as I write, I think she would be saying: " Yes—but it was all Henry— make it clear how calm *he* was ": and looking at my book on H.I., which she did not live to see, she would say, " You have done so "—and then she would add: " What is there to say about me ?—I was ever a very useful actress."

She was very fond of that little phrase—for she was *very useful*—no better definition of a good actress could be made.

I remember only one other actress who has ever struck me as " *very useful* "—her name is Campagna. The second of two sisters—she played with Angelo Musco, the Sicilian comedian of genius. Father and mother and an elder (or younger) sister acted with her: she always took the smaller parts— but by Jove, what a good actress—faultless. Ever useful and at every moment—never out of place—never out of tune—never out of time—she was the thing itself. The whole family was obviously born to act—none of them but was first-class— but she was even more than that. She and E.T. were as like as two pins—no, as two flowers.

And what can you write about two flowers, which grow by the grace of nature ? The critic instantly

H

thinks of half a brick—he'd find something to say, once the brick comes to mind. It's an obsession, that brick. But when the critics went to the Lyceum, they very often had to admit that E.T. disarmed them, and they never drew their brick.

Or rather, they never heaved it at her. They were defeated and delightful men, delighted to pass the brick into their left hands and hurl it at Irving . . . what? not at Irving? well then, at Terriss— no, Terriss looked too handsome to deserve more than a couple of mild adjectives . . . at Tyars, at Conway, at Alexander, at that young and conceited Gordon Craig.

Wallop!

The trouble of carrying a brick to a theatre is that it's got to be flung at someone. Meantime, critics, some necessary question of the play is then to be considered—not to do so is villainous. But who among us artists or actors will cast the first pebble back at you? First of all we have not the skill, and we haven't the pebble handy.

THE day-time rehearsals were not more delightful than those held at night—and I can remember night rehearsals which began for the whole company at about eight, and went on to three or four in the morning: but whether a rehearsal or a performance hardly mattered—all that counts is the place, the stage—its greenroom, passages and costumes, its scenes and lights—and its curtain. The stage and curtain matter most.

There is much written to-day about the audience—its psychology, and so forth. To us of the Lyceum, all that mattered were the stalls, the pit and the gallery. These we thought of as places—just as soldiers of old thought of bastion, keep and court-yard. These places were to us the things to capture.

"The pit rose at me," said Kean—he didn't refer to the people, but to the place.

The great actor considers the house—and by the sensitive scales of his secret nature, he weighs the house. As the curtain rises, as he utters his first words, he knows his pit and his gallery—later on is time enough for his stalls.

IN our house, the Lyceum, I lived over on one side of the big glade, my mother on the other. I was on P., she on O.P. side. The Prompter was the source of these denominations.

At the Lyceum he was on the right side of the stage—the spectator's right—and flat against the proscenium. The Prompter was Mr. Allen.

So that right side was called the Prompt side, and

the other side the Opposite Prompt side—i.e., P. and O.P.

On the Prompt side were the two Greenrooms, where the actors went to look at themselves in the long pier-glasses, instead of having to go back to their dressing-rooms, which might be far away from the stage. At the Lyceum the best dressing-rooms were near the stage, the worst were up one, two, and three flights of stairs—rather narrow stairs —old-fashioned, Dickens-like stairs. The six to eight dressing-rooms downstairs were used by the chief actor—Forbes-Robertson, Terriss or Alexander, as the case might be—and most of the chief actresses —two or three actresses in each room. Upstairs, in the end room on the second floor, Pinero, Cooper and Norman Forbes dressed: John Archer, Tyars, Haviland and Martin Harvey on the third, I think —and so forth: and it was up these stairs I would bolt as soon as my work was done.

On this side of the Theatre was also the property room, and one of the largest of the several scene-docks; and upstairs, Hawes Craven's large scene-painting studio, and the Beef Steak Room.

That is about all there was on the Prompt side of the stage. On the O.P., on the ground floor, were the administration offices—two small rooms

—the long passage leading up to the Royal Box; and upstairs, the wardrobe rooms, and Irving's dressing-room and Ellen Terry's dressing-room.

IT is a queer experience, this dressing and undressing in a Theatre, for a costume piece as it is called; but one only realizes how odd it is long after one has left the stage.

We go down to the Theatre, arriving at about seven o'clock—an hour before the curtain is to rise—and pass into our dressing-room. Our dresser takes our hat and coat and hangs them up, and we then begin to put off the dusty clothes of our real existence, and to look at ourselves in the looking-glass, which has one or two or more lights—movable, if we are lucky—around it. We put on tights or breeches and stockings, according to the period—*Hamlet* or *Faust* or *Charles Surface*. Then we draw up before the glass, and begin to dress our face. We generally make ourselves look as charming as possible, or else impossibly hideous . . . or rather we did—for I speak of my own time, 1889 to 1897.

Nowadays we are grown much cleverer—more subtle—more artistic—which is just as well: it was a long-felt want on our part to get on, to advance, to develop; and at the Lyceum some of us even wanted to do ourselves justice, to shine in the eyes of the Governor—H.I. Yet what assistant actor in his senses would attempt to do himself justice, to shine, in the eyes of Henry Irving? The best he could do would be to keep his great talent from outshining the Chief—and keep out of his light— and remember his lines.

Democracy, in those days, did not mean making yourself a damn nuisance to your employer.

As for showing up well before Ellen Terry, and getting a good word from her, that was not difficult —but what was difficult to avoid was the kind look that accompanied it.

But she had a distinct appreciation of the work of some of the actors.

Terriss she always laughed at—not because he was at all laughable to the audience, but because he was so very simple in his methods—spoke out, looked fierce—gay—offended—distrait—and always handsome—but never looked particularly tragic or comic—never seemed to be an actor. His first words in one part would be delivered in the same tone as his last, and would differ but slightly from the tones in all his parts. But E. T. always appreciated his clear-cut way of doing and saying things; and since character and passion were to be of no account with him, nothing could be better.

For the work of Norman Forbes she had a considerable appreciation: when he played *Shylock* to her *Portia*, she wrote me that it was really admirable: his *Student* in "Faust," his *Andrew Aguecheek*, his *Dogberry*, were among a whole string of performances which no one could deny were about as good as they could possibly be.

I think he was the first to play *Moses* to her *Olivia*—and this was a part I played when he was no longer with us at the Lyceum.

And I was thinking of this part when I began to describe the oddity of dressing up in a Theatre. I liked that eighteenth century suit of clothes very much. It consisted of brown breeches and coat, a striped waistcoat, black shoes with buckles, and a plain and well used black three cornered hat.

I HAVE the breeches and stockings on, and the plain shirt, without frills, but soft and not starched—with something plain in the way of frills at the wrist—and I am making up. I know my part, of course—all the rehearsals are over and done with—and though we have played several plays since, when we come to do "Olivia" again (we did it fairly often) we still know our parts. I liked *Moses* —it was easy to play it, and I had some scenes with H. I.

As soon as dressed, I'd take my hat, and leaving the room I would go downstairs, walk onto the glorious stage—with the lights quite low still, for the curtain wouldn't be up for fifteen minutes—and, going through the porch of the Vicarage, I would make my way to the staircase which led to H. I.'s room, and, further along, to E. T.'s.

Dressed as *Moses* I would knock and go in, and find Nelly, my mother, very much Nelly, because it was one of her earliest parts, in which she achieved great success: and there she was, settling on her *Olivia* cap—a beautiful thing—and looking at herself, and generally entering the part.

Always rather nervous before the piece began, she talked little at such times—but generally wanted to have a look at me . . . so I stood there and looked at myself in her tall glass, and she looked at me.

There's a lot of looking in the looking-glass goes on in a theatre—a tremendous lot. One doesn't come into another fellow's dressing-room and sit down and look at him—one comes in, and at once looks in the looking-glass. There one is sure to find his reflection—and the reflection is very much more to us than the solid thing itself. So we stand

and talk to each other's reflection—and go on looking at ourselves.

Irving, meantime, in the next room, is making up methodically—silently . . . murmuring to some visitor who may be seated in a chair: " Yes, the part of *Olivia* is one of the most re*mark*able which that heaven*sent actress, Ellen Terry, has ever blessed us with."

I GO downstairs after I have inspected E.T. in the mirrors—and I find the stage full of characters and character. *Old Burchell; Squire Thornhill;* Arnott, the property*man—whose apple tree in that scene was a masterpiece of realism; *Polly Flamborough,* in blue and pink; Meredith Ball, the musical conductor, in evening dress; some villagers; all a mix*up of eighteenth and nineteenth century . . . actors in eighteenth, and scene*shifters and Prompter and others in nineteenth.

Soon comes E.T.; then H.I., dressed in his clericals, attended by Loveday and his dresser—who carries a tray with a modicum of make*up and other necessities.

E.T.'s dresser plants herself by the side, ready for E.T.'s first exit, when she may need a dab here or a dab there.

And now the orchestra begins to tune up—and

Terriss is looking through the hole in the centre of the curtain—a rolling curtain—and seeing whom he can recognize in front. I do so too—we all do it—we rake the stalls and dress circle and boxes with our one eye—we see no one we can recognize as a personal friend, or we see one—perhaps two—twenty or more if it's a first night. But as our personal friend has not seen us, our glimpse was in the nature of spying: we have taken whatever advantage was to be had—though when we turn away from the curtain, and once more see the village of Wakefield—its apple tree, Vicarage, and the old Manor House a mile or two off on Craven's back-cloth—we have utterly forgotten our friend. This is how it seemed to me, for I was not yet fifty-five—I am then only twenty-two.

The music in the orchestra, which consists mainly of old English song-tunes strung together, is coming to an end—the Prompter claps his hands—the lights are turned up and on, and we all flow rapidly off the stage into our positions, leaving the youngsters who begin the piece marooned in the centre . . . they glance slyly at each other to see if the other is nervous, or showing nervousness, for of course their hearts are beating twice the pace.

There is a pause—the lights in the front of the house are being turned down very slowly—the orchestra starts once the old dance tune of " Sir Roger de Coverley," *pianissimo*, and up rolls the huge curtain as easily as say Shaw.

But Shaw didn't write this version of " The Vicar of Wakefield "—Wills, another Irishman, did—wrote it from a pretty good story by Goldsmith, another Irishman, who had a pretty skilled hand, with apparently genius, brains galore, little bitterness, and no vanity: unaware of the coming of Count Tolstoi (not an Irishman) or of Bolshevism—even innocent that in fifteen years' time France would start chopping off good men's heads to the tune of " Ça ira."

The tune of " Ça ira " would take up the curtain of " The Vicar of Wakefield" if played in Leningrad to-day—but, as I say, " Sir Roger de Coverley " took it up in 1890. Such a vast difference.

The stage-management of this first act of this play was a nice rhythmical piece of work: by that I mean not too brainy—not too deucedly clever— clever enough, and flowing.

It was to a great extent due to John Hare, who had produced it in 1878 at the Court Theatre, and from whom H.I. had taken a good deal of the " business "—for Ellen Terry had been the centre of the Court Theatre production, and carried with her to the Lyceum the spirit of the first production.

Hare was a remarkable producer of a play, and we are told by E.T. in her memoirs that he " produced 'Olivia' perfectly." Irving added to his production, and E.T. gave it the rhythm it needed.

In this play I could seldom see my mother's performance of the famous Act II, because I would be on the stage at the time—up at the back of the scene, and talking to Irving. Our conversation was hushed—our movements silent, and reduced to a very few—we went on with all the power of the engines shut off and silenced, the plane just gliding on. For the least click of noise, the least jerk of movement from those of us at the back of a stage, can ruin the work being done by the actors in front of us, and who are carrying the weight of the whole drama in their hands at the moment.

III

WHEN the play was over and the stage scene struck—the pieces put away—the lights put out, all but a few which burned on dimly—the actors all dressed in their world clothes, and gone home— I would once more descend the old stairs and cross the stage and go up to E.T.'s dressing-room.

Often people would have delayed her by coming round to see her and to talk. It seems an unkind thing to do—to go round to talk to a performer who is dead tired after having acted, sung or danced for about two hours: and it's a queer notion to expect to find *Olivia* and Ellen Terry by going round, when you could never find them together except by sitting in front.

E.T., once rid of her kind friends, would bustle along and be dressed in no time, and we would descend to the private entrance, and find there the carriage with the sticks laid across from seat to seat, and she would get in and lie down at once.

I would get in and sit up—but I used to be so tired that I was fast asleep before we had reached Pall Mall.

Arriving at Barkston Gardens, I would get out, open the door, come back to help E.T. out, tell the coachman what time he would be needed next day; and as he pulled away from the house, we would be closing and bolting the front door and entering the cheery dining-room, where a good—a very good—meal awaited us.

E.T. in her book says I was " a greedy little thing " at four years old: but I wasn't a scrap less so at twenty—and to-day, if I go to lunch at Larue's or Claridge's, it is not because I am convinced it is the right thing to do, but because I am greedy.

Now E.T. was just the same: she did not guzzle, but she never failed to enjoy the food which waited for us each night after the show. If it were summer time, it would be all spread out on the table and sideboard; if in winter, it would be standing before a glowing fire in its different dishes. No one ever sat up for us, and we were quite happy to help ourselves.

At these suppers, I sat at the head of the table, and E.T. sat at my right hand. She never sat at the head of her table until she moved to King's Road, Chelsea.

At lunch—which we called dinner, since it took place at about two o'clock or two-thirty—we assembled round the table as in the diagram:—

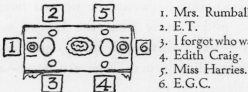

1. Mrs. Rumball, called "Boo."
2. E.T.
3. I forgot who was here—some lady.
4. Edith Craig.
5. Miss Harries.
6. E.G.C.

I think I have it right, but I am quite sure of numbers 1, 2 and 6, and the point is to show where E.T. placed herself. It is little things like this that say such a lot, when voices are too faint to carry—distances too great.

So we, Boo and I, the eldest and the youngest, took the head and foot of the table. She was my rival, and well I had bedevilled her when I gave her the nickname of "Boo." Isn't it strange that besides most of the best tunes, some of the happiest names are dedicated to Old Nick? It is, strangely enough, to Gods that mankind has always offered up the best oaths . . . proof positive, somehow, of our eternal trust in God.

Boo was my rival, for she, too, carved a joint or a chicken at her end of the table. I was the real carver, because a woman can rarely carve. Mother could, and taught me. She was a good craftsman, as a glance at her rather large, but white and speaking hands revealed.

I never knew such a pair of hands—like a physiognomy, they lighted up with expression—looked all sorts of things—and belonged somehow to so long ago. Useful as she made them, they were so much more than that . . . they were indeed beautiful. Not only because of their expression, I think—I cannot tell for certain—but I think they were lovely in themselves. In repose—closed across her breast, they still seemed alive—the hands of *Beatrice*, *Imogen* and *Portia's* right hand.

She could play the piano well—she touched the notes with much surety, and without assault: her hands could grasp without snatching—ward without a tremor—hold firmly, ready to let go at the first sign—and hold up, sign or no sign.

All her life lay in these strange, fine hands—and when she held the carving fork and knife and showed me how to cut a leg of mutton or a sirloin of beef, I learnt from her performance in a trice. If only Blake's sheep had been as real as the mutton, and the tuition the same—the craftsman's teaching!

So my rival, Boo, was in a few days utterly worsted, when, at seventeen, I began to carve the handsome joints of those days, and do it generously, if with a little guile. You who carve, will know what I mean: we carvers do help the others, since we cannot help ourselves, first; and we do try to give them the best pieces; but we do also manage, at the same time, to cut little bits and let them fall to Lazarus' share— our share—leaving them in the dish, as we carve our way to the satisfaction of everyone.

But mother was greedy—and her greediness taught me the best bits. When I began on the mutton's leg, first the ancient Boo would be served, then E.T., then Edith, then Miss Harries, and lastly, of course, myself. But by the time I had come to E.T., and her eye detected the exact curve I was giving to the knife—the very twist I had put on the fork—she would rise, come round behind me, and positively point rudely to the bits she wanted.

What is the tenderest bit in the centre of the leg called—the sort of undercut of the leg?—"There—there," she would say, and soon I learnt: and then that special little piece of brown fat (every gourmet will know which)—it had to be sliced off and go onto her plate; and then she was satisfied, and marched off with it in triumph.

That's about all she got out of playing *Portia* and *Ophelia* for two hundred and fifty nights.

I would serve her properly ever after—but I gave a glance at the faces and hands of the others, and rightly or wrongly came to the conclusion that they were not as worthy of the tit-bits as she. After about six months, and I carving on and on, day after day, it dawned on me that they even despised these delicacies. So I would try first one inferior slice on one of them, then another, and with a casual request here and there as to whether they thought the meat tender, I soon discovered that they were one and all devoid of taste.

My sister, with a sententiousness which always passed as wisdom with my mother, would also occasionally rise up and direct my operations. It was a comic performance, but for all this gave my mother serious pangs of delight, and did me

I

no harm. I managed quite easily to get the next best bits after the host.

And at supper, when E.T. and I got home, we kept to the same seats—I at the foot of the table, and she at the side; or she slid down and took the place where at the luncheon-dinner Miss Harries always sat—on my right.

Of the estimable—the dear—Miss Harries, I shall write in another book. She looked after the house: she was so odd to look at, but to be looked after by this faint, transparent, shrimp-like little person, was to be looked after by an energetic little angel.

Enough of her, and of Boo, until to-morrow: to-day it's night—it's half-past twelve by now, and Mother and I seated at our table—all very silent, and I about to fall asleep once more.

For, tired after the evening of acting, of changing and rechanging from one's supposed real self into the far greater reality of *Moses* or *Oswald* or *Cromwell*, I soon found the warm room and food gaining control over me, and a heaviness would begin to trouble my head—for Mother sat fairly silent—I cannot recall anything she said.

She had eight or ten letters on her plate—fourteen or fifteen had come to the Theatre that evening— she had opened and read them and brought them home . . . and now these others—mostly as dull as ditchwater.

But one letter was always there, after 1892, and this was generally a fairly long letter. Do not suppose that I am coming yet to Mr. Bernard Shaw, who in 1892 began to write to her—the one letter which always came was from Miss Marmonnier.

Who was Miss Marmonnier, that she should take precedence of G.B.S.? Well, she was all that he was not: she was small, she was shy, she dressed in black, she paid for her seats to see her idol, Ellen Terry—she went nearly every night—she was up in the gallery—and she would write letter after letter to E.T., saying in her unliterary way how much she adored her . . . that the great pleasure she derived was impossible to express, and that she hoped Miss Terry was well, and she feared she would tire herself if not careful, and that she would write again another day. She never asked for anything— she wanted nothing—she was a good little woman.

Actresses are bored to death by the type of person who writes these long letters to them day by day, and yet it attracts them—actresses are not very much cleverer than the rest of humanity—and when Miss Marmonnier used to write to Ellen Terry day by day, letters of three to five pages long, Ellen Terry read them, not impatiently but with a certain pleasure to think that here was one of her admirers who, though badly off, paid to sit night after night in the gallery, who night after night listened and wept and laughed and then applauded, who took and gave pleasure, and who now was helping her to realize that so it was.

Miss Marmonnier must have been French; and in her speech she hesitated, just as she did in her boldest actions; but she was sincere, and I came to know this queer little ancient person, and to like her—and even rescued her once from a rather awkward predicament. Of that I shall write a little when I come to the immortal figures of Miss Harries and Boo—I mean they are to me immortal.

But Miss Marmonnier wrote a lot—long letters —just praises, turned and returned, first one way, then another, and in their own way a song.

G. B. S. never sang. And so, on hearing that all his letters were being collected and prettily harmonized so as to issue them in a big book (poor mother —how she would have loathed it !) I bethought me of that other, lesser, better writer—dear little Miss Marmonnier. I enquired at the right source for information as to whether anyone had come across her letters—possibly several hundred. No—not a letter from Miss Marmonnier had been preserved —none were to be found. How like kind Fate !

Then it rests with me to testify to the existence of this little woman—to make for her a tiny niche into which, like a mouse, she will creep right enough, harming no one. And I do so here—have done it —it has only taken a few moments; and I place her niche, figure and all, by the side of the cabinet photograph of G. B. S., with the request that any other genuine theatre-lover, theatre-goer, gallery first-nighter or pittite, will guard her and see she gets a place always. One never knows whether famous people with elbows won't try to push an unknown out of the way.

I WAS asleep at the table and nodding forwards, by the time E. T. came to tear open her G. B. S. letter. She did now and again say something about these letters which came, but I'm afraid all she said was lost on me. Sleep is so much more powerful than words.

But do not sleep, reader, till we go upstairs, my mother and I. Kind to me as ever, she finishes her supper quickly, and, gathering her bulky hand-bag, her cloak, and goodness knows what not else, asks, as she reaches the foot of the stairs, if I have turned off the light in the hall—bolted the front door ? I have, and I have managed to put on the chain— and now the lights over the old supper table are put out, and another in the hall, and she turns to go up—and I behind, to help her by pushing. Such long stairs, and she so tired, and I not tired, but so sleepy.

Yet there are but three flights to go, and so up we go—lights out—lights out again—passing the closed doors of dark rooms where others sleep.

Now she is in her own room—and " good night," she says—and she will potter around for awhile— and I go up one more flight, and put out another light; and I undress for the third or fourth time that evening, turn out the last light, and roll into bed, asleep—fast asleep already. No more dreams, no more nightmares of my childhood—no more dread—all gone, because of the Theatre, the supper, the Theatre, the undressing, the Theatre, the work —and the Mother.

NELLY AND E. T. AGAIN QUARREL

I REMAINED acting with my mother at the Lyceum Theatre for about eight years. I left the Lyceum in 1897, and stopped acting altogether at the end of the same year.

Of this my mother writes a few lines in her memoirs (1908):—" *It had been a great grief to me when I lost my son as an actor.*" She adds something about my talents.

I know what she means—and I, too, grieved that I could not go on acting. What actor of twenty-five years old, who had played with H. I. and E. T. would not ? Besides, I had played some bigger parts in other theatres during the Lyceum vacation months—I had acted *Romeo*, *Petruchio*, *Charles Surface*, *Young Marlow*, *Macbeth*, and *Hamlet*.

Acting these, I discovered that I was not a second Irving. Returning to the Lyceum, I discovered why. This settled it for me, and I silently determined anyhow to be *some*body and do *some*thing.

I looked around me: " What," I asked myself, " What still remains to be done in this world of the Theatre, where all seems to me to be so perfect ? "

This question teased me for several years—for the last two years at the Lyceum, and for two years after I had left.

Ellen Terry was not urging me to act—she naturally did not use her influence to persuade theatre people that I was a marvellous actor—she did not inspire me or tempt me, as a Mephista would have done, by a real good dose of flattery. I could have done with it, for I was quite convinced that I was not a good actor—whereas it seems that up to a point I was quite passable at the craft. But when I watched H. I. in the last act of " The Lyons Mail " and in " The Bells," I felt that beyond that there was no going, and I told myself that I could either be content for the rest of my life to follow Irving and become a feeble imitation of him, or discover who I was and be that. So I made my choice, and I turned my back on Irving for many a year—occasionally looking over my shoulder to catch one more look at the loved figure.

I went right away—it is called hardening the heart; it certainly meant keeping a very stiff upper lip. I began to read books which were very critical of stage players and play-acting, and contemptuous of the theatrical. I was surprised to learn how many wise men had given the theatre and all pertaining to it a very severe dressing.

I was astounded and furious, at first, with these traducers of our noble profession, our sacred calling, our Art. But after a while I began to discover that, dash it all, if these men could speak so gravely, there must be *something* in what they said.

Goethe, Nietzsche, Lamb, Coleridge, Ruskin, Tolstoi, Wagner—I was beginning to read what they had to say. And I became attentive.

I had attended until then to no one but Irving—the headmaster of my preparatory school: but now, as it were, I was at College, and the solemn thinkers of the ages, all new to me, came in in cap and gown, silently took their seats.

I was in this sense self-taught.

Slowly something began to dawn—I caught a glimmering of something—that was all I could say —and went off to the Museums to acquire a bit of practical knowledge. I lost much time pottering over costume—it was the last of the Lyceum influences hanging round me. And I gave time to drawing—I call it drawing, but it was with me something more like a bad habit—always sketching things into a note-book, at the National Gallery or when out for a walk, and puzzling over a theatre which should be more real—yes, that was it —more real than the old Lyceum had been. It had not yet occurred to me (or to anyone else) that if a theatre were *less* real than the Lyceum, that would be really getting at something along quite a different path, and lead somewhere.

But this idea did come to me within a year or so. I had not heard of anyone but Wagner and the Meiningen Company as having done anything exceptional in the continental theatre. And Wagner interested me. His productions, I mean, for his music I could not understand, though I enjoyed hearing it. His productions were interesting mainly for the fact that I noted that he laid down the theory (carried into practice by his assistants) that the music-drama of the Future (the word thrilled me—one last glance back over my shoulder at H. I.) deserved at least a new sort of theatre of its own. A new building, of a shape quite new ! Really this was very interesting—I drew up my chair closer to the table, and read all that was in the book about this new shape of the Wagner theatre that was already in existence at Bayreuth. I looked long and long at the plans—" Um-m," said I to myself, as I rose and went out, satisfied that here was an Idea worthy of the theatre.

But that fellow Nietzsche ! damn him—for his attack on Wagner—for his impertinence to all theatres—for his contempt for the actor. Let's

look at him again and see what he really has
to say.

I looked again, and became livid with fury. . . .
He was actually right !

Never mind—leave it—leave Nietzsche, come to
him later—get on. New shape of a theatre—that is
in any case a sensible notion. New shape of place
suggests new world, leads pleasantly enough to new
colours—gives us new points of view, takes the mind
away from the theatre of do-as-was-done-last-time.
Someone then told me that at Hengler's Circus,
in 1886—that was but thirteen years from the time
I am speaking of—my father had transformed
the Circus into a Greek Theatre,[1] giving a quite
new shape to the stage. A long, and not very
high proscenium—but the eye could go up, following the high lines *behind* the proscenium—few
borders or flapping cloths—that's original.

" I'll inherit that," I thought . . . it seemed to
me to be quite a big fortune.

Get away from the hypnotic force of the old
shapes, colours, rhymes and reasons, and you will
then feel free to create something fresh.

So I reasoned—and E. T. could not make out
what was going on in me.

[1] Reproduced in *Gordon Craig and the Theatre*, by Enid Rose
(Sampson Low).

I saw her seldom now; I lived in the country, and she lived in London, at Barkston Gardens or King's Road, Chelsea—or in America—having to play in pieces like "Madame sans Gêne," "The Medicine Man," and "Robespierre." And Bernard Shaw was writing to her at this time, urging her to leave Henry Irving and be damned to the Lyceum—which was not good advice, was quite absurd, and was also not without a tinge of self-interest—and for these reasons, should never have been given.

I went here and there, reading, drawing and puzzling things out; and by chance one day, towards the end of 1898, I met a musician—a composer of music—Martin Shaw. Martin is in no way related to Bernard.

In 1899, Martin Shaw told me he was getting together a chorus to sing Purcell's "Dido and Æneas," he had founded "The Purcell Operatic Society," at Hampstead, at the suggestion of Mrs. Dryhurst. He invited me to help him—I was delighted—for I always preferred to practise, rather than to theorize: and so we began to rehearse the thing as a dramatic performance.

Martin Shaw has told about this in his book, *Up to Now*[1] ; what he has not told is the sort of nature that is his. I shall try to describe him in my

[1] Published by the Oxford University Press.

next book; here I can only say that he was buoyant
and a good sportsman—the best I have known. It
was as easy to hunt the Purcell, the theatre, the
critics and the public with him, as to go out on the
moors for a good day's shooting.

The opera, "Dido and Æneas," was prepared by us
and by our seventy to eighty helpers, in the autumn
of 1899, all of us working for nothing—all but the
leading lady and a few principal singers: and in
May, 1900, we put it on at the then Hampstead
Conservatoire, now the Embassy Theatre. We
made our proscenium: we practically built our
stage: an odd shape, larger and not quite like any
that had been used; and the show was odd too—we
didn't try to make it odd—I'm only reporting what
people thought of it. The singers did marvels—
and, to come to Hecuba, we seem to have done
something rather new in the way of theatricals: and
there was no deficit.

MY mother was away in America when we gave
the opera; and though one or two people
wrote to her about it, they probably explained little.
She returned to London while we were preparing
a second piece—"The Masque of Love," as we
called it, from Purcell's " Dioclesian."

I did my part of this better than I had done " Dido

and Æneas"; and Ellen Terry, in order to give our new efforts a helping hand, allowed us to announce that "Dido and Æneas" and "The Masque of Love" would be preceded by "Nance Oldfield," which E. T. had made into a marvellously attractive thing. We opened and played for a week at the Coronet Theatre, Notting Hill Gate. Our expenses were just about covered by our takings.

E. T. saw these two pieces, I think. What she thought about them, I am not sure. Somehow it really never seemed to me to matter what she thought, for I knew that about a thing done by someone she loved she could not think straight, and would never be able to express—who can when they like a thing very much? She was all for what she liked—and then, on top of her liking, she could and would be quite critical.

I HAVE had to relate as briefly as possible all this about my first two productions of 1900 and 1901, and how they came about, and what was the effect of their reception on me, for it all leads up to the reaction this had upon my mother Nelly. She had been grieved that I had thrown up acting, and felt that it meant throwing up the theatre. She had lifted that lovely hand of hers to shade her eyes from the glare of things, and searched to find me. " Where is he going ? " she said in her far-away voice, " I can't see him ": but now she began to see, and almost realized what it meant.

It revived her to hear of my production of " Dido and Æneas "—she was keenly interested (as well as excited) witnessing " The Masque "—but for all this, she could not, and she *would* not let herself realize what it all meant.

For she knew that it meant a long fight for me against odds, plenty of heartbreak, for the coming thirty years. To her, as to many sensible people, a deliberate going against the public, even if you had a few staunch critics and friends with you, meant courting failure and asking for a modern martyrdom. That is precisely what it has meant, and I preferred it to a cheap success.

So I was out for the fight of a lifetime, and E. T., without daring to tell herself so, and thrice her head thus waving up and down, smiled and tried to look happy.

As time went on, she grew happier about it all, because by 1909–12 Europe and America were all in favour of the idea, and were making it pay hand over fist. So it was not to the discredit of Ellen

Terry after all—the credit is due to her. . . and the cash goes to Europe and America.

BUT before that time was reached she and I came to work once more together. It was in 1903, and it happened this way:

The Lyceum Theatre had closed its doors in 1902, and H. I. and E. T. never more acted together, except in the United States, and in the provinces, and that only for a short time longer.

In the same year, 1902, I produced "Bethlehem" and also "Acis and Galatea," and over the latter I had a fall.

I lost money. Martin Shaw was with me, and he did all he could to prevent a catastrophe—but we went with a crash. No vast sum was involved—but no one would foot even our deficit of about £400—we asked five or six wealthy people—times were as bad then as in 1931—times so often are, with people who have money. So I had to pay it off myself. It took some time, but I did it without resorting to the fashionable dodge of the Bankruptcy courts.

My mother was away in America, and did not see the work; but on her return, she advanced me the money, so that I could pay the debts of "Acis and Galatea"—and then, a year later, arranged for me to produce "The Vikings" and "Much Ado About Nothing," for which I was paid a quarter of my salary, the other three-quarters of it going to repay her the advances she had made.[1]

And now for a few remembrances of this, our last work together—"The Vikings" and "Much Ado about Nothing," at the Imperial Theatre—and of the quarrel between E. T. and Nelly, my mother.

AT the Imperial Theatre there was no business management to speak of. What E. T. needed and what the originality of the venture needed, owing to its risky nature, was a little real first-class organization. No organizer was with us. This was the main error. I doubt if there was one man in the whole theatrical world of England at that time with sufficient moral courage and intelligence to handle the business side of the venture. In Germany there were a few such men, as I found out on going over there six months later.

We started out without a play—we relied on the name ELLEN TERRY with its immense drawing

[1] She had left Irving in 1903. It will be seen that here was an excellent opportunity for the author of "Candida" to suggest something—he didn't—he had no suggestion to make, and no theatre. So much for all the talk about it in his letters. But Beerbohm Tree did, and she joined him, and playing *Mrs. Page* in "The Merry Wives of Windsor," did the last and best work of her career—for in "The Vikings," "The Good Hope," "Alice Sit by the Fire" and "Captain Brassbound's Conversion," she was not as magnificent as she was as *Mrs. Page* . . . I think "magnificent" is the word. Charming she was, later, in "Pinkie and he Fairies," and noble in *Hermione* and then that was all.

K

capacity to fill a theatre which was rather out of the way . . . it was down in Westminster, and off the beaten track, and London people did not know how to get to it. The advertising was inadequate, so that people would always be asking " Where is the Imperial, and how is it reached ? "

The building itself—the work of the architect, Verity—was admirable in many ways. It was very handsome, with a rather poor façade and an insig-nificant entrance—but inside, it had a real beauty. Not small—not too large—and with a stage adequate in the old-fashioned way of 1900. I was quite content with the stage, and even its inadequate lighting equipment would do.

What was not bad was the company of actors. We had Norman Forbes and Holman Clarke, Mr. and Mrs. Matheson Lang, one of the Tearles, Har-court Williams and Hubert Carter: Charles Terry was with us too. But there was an obstructionist in our midst—a foreigner, who played one of the most important parts.

There was another obstructionist—one of the chief workers in the costume department, which was under the direction of my sister.

For Edith Craig had a genius for theatrical costume—and E. T. had set her up in good and central organization in Henrietta Street some years previous to this—probably in 1895 or '6 . . . anyhow, Edith Craig had, by hard work and perseverance, added to a very considerable talent, achieved an enviable position as a costume expert— making these and sometimes designing them, it was admitted, better than anyone else in London.

Under her direction were made all the costumes for "The Vikings," and, I believe, for "Much Ado About Nothing."

I LOOKED forward to the collaboration of my costumière sister in this production, for till then I had not been able to count on much professional assistance in that difficult department in my previous productions. I thought that when she and my mother and myself got to work, we should be able to defy all the intrigue of the theatre and do something so much worth while, that within two or three years—for I supposed we should keep on and see it through— we should have established a permanent Theatre in London of value to the dramatic art and profitable to our family as well.

But this obstructionist in the costume department had a devil in her, and managed so to upset Ellen Terry and to play people one against the other, that our fortunes and the fortunes of the Imperial venture began to look dark at once.

E. T. was the commander-in-chief, and she hadn't the strength or experience of one: she had always relied on H. I. to command. She should have sacked four people in the company before the first week of rehearsals was over, but she couldn't bring herself to do anything so positive.

To illustrate how well she realized that she couldn't take and hold a point of view, two extracts from letters written about 1918–1919 will serve.[1] The first was written to me, the second to Sir Albert Seymour, who has kindly allowed me to use it:

1. To me: " . . . Folk want me to vote—*I won't*—a dangerous thing to do without knowledge—I love loyalty to the King that is set up—believe, however, that *in my heart* I am a *good* democrat—but oh, I see *this* way and *that* way—and a *wobbler* like that does mischief. I'm not clever. I'm a fool. —So knowing Fools are very dangerous in times like these, I shall leave it to old Edy and Co. who will plump of course for Labour . . ."

2. To Sir Albert Seymour: "You constantly remind me of you by your constant little kindnesses and we very often speak of you. Somehow, altho' we 'hung out Banners on the outward walls,' the *Peace* news seems to fall very flat— we have frightful discussions at the Cottage about the general hang of things politically, and old C. . . . gets purple and blue and Edy backs her up. It's awfully funny—for altho' I go a great distance with them, I draw the line at the extermination of Ll.G. and the Universe—. . . . . —*I don't* think everyone is just as good as another,

[1] See also Frontispiece to the Annex.

and that Jack's as good as his Master—It was never intended. I certainly *do* think a really FINE *Democrat* is a splendid article, but I like *gentle people*, gentle manners, and the old old Ideals to be carried on and handed down and reverenced—. . . . ."

It was this inability to take a definite stand with decision, which brought about the failure of that venture at the Imperial Theatre, which might otherwise have developed into a permanent and profitable institution.

SO the intriguing member of the wardrobe department stayed on. I think she is not to be held entirely responsible for her devilry—for she had become one of the suffragettes—she could not see as the rest of the world saw. She saw women as angels come direct from a heaven one cut above that heaven inhabited by God. She saw men as demons come from a hell far worse than that where Satan hung out. She was quite convinced. She would flare up, for no reason, about the cut of a cloak or the colour of a cloth, and anathematize me and all the male members of the company, because we were at that moment not entirely agreeing with her: she took it as an insult to the whole sex that we should dare to suggest that she could possibly make a mistake. God might err, but no woman could. "Yes—yes—it is—it is a direct and cowardly attack on the suffragettes——" and she would glare and snap.

But why did not Ellen Terry sack her at once, and in this way save the whole important venture; and why did not E. T. also sack the foreign gentleman? And why did she not ask one of her city friends for some youngish live-wire of a business man to replace the man of affairs who was muddling things? He was quite an able man—he could have run any ordinary venture excellently, for he was one of those men who let a thing run itself: but this Imperial Theatre venture was a bit exceptional—it was difficult but well worth the consideration and application of a young business man with the determination to see the thing through to a triumph. For we held good cards—it only needed a bit of business acumen to play them well.

BUT this could not be, for here lay the trouble. E. T. and my mother Nelly were once more at loggerheads.

It was I who had selected the piece—Ibsen's "Vikings." It was a bad choice—and the mother made the first error in agreeing to this. She agreed to it because her son wanted it—which is no good reason at all—for she wasn't well suited to the chief part in "The Vikings," and people would not want to see her in " such a horrid character "; and the whole drawing-power of the venture at the start, lay with her.

No one in England but a very few thousand people cared two straws for any art of any theatre: all the larger public cared for, the 400,000, was to go and see " dear Ellen Terry," and this larger public was the fellow who was to pay for the venture.

So why did not E. T. think in her accustomed wise and practical way (I think I hear her saying, " Oh Ted, I'm not wise, I'm not practical ") and select some comedy and a company of good comedians to play it with her, and allow me the first or the last three quarters of an hour to do some of my kind of work? If she had done that, she would have had no need even to engage the foreigner—Norwegian, I believe he was—though she would certainly have had to sack the costumière—and then the Business Manager would only have had to sit still and count the dollars as they rolled in over him.

No old piece would have done: neither would a new play by Bernard Shaw, for England isn't the continent, and while his plays were occupying many people's attention in Europe, only his Jaegers and vegetarianism were at that time of interest to the Britons, who, besides all that, swore daily that they never, never could possibly be slaves, and were morally and intellectually slaves to public opinion every hour of the year—what a blessing all that has passed !

E. T. at the Imperial Theatre, presenting "The Vikings" to the London of 1903 which didn't want Ibsen and loathed to see E. T. in a "wicked woman's part," was a grievous spectacle: and my way of producing a play or an opera attracted very few people in England at that time. Artists, and a few hundred others were interested, and a thousand or so might have been quite willing to pay for seats to see what I had to give them— but in 1903 you couldn't run a full-sized playhouse on the strength of a couple of thousand eager enthusiasts.

Ellen Terry began to get anxious and then more anxious: she called the dear public all sorts of names —she thought them " fools, utter fools, not to care a scrap about what is fine." She had often damned them behind their backs; though when she heard their applause ringing in her ears, she was of course persuaded that they had remarkable discernment— one always is.

"The Vikings" was only fairly well advertised, though it lent itself to some first-class publicity: still, to advertise in London, so as to be effective, costs a very great deal of money—it must have cost E. T. much more than the mere lighting and production costs, but she does not touch on that in her book: her manager possibly only drew her attention to my mote of a bill, not to his own beaming one. My production expenses were comparatively little—one of the largest scenes only cost £100, I remember—and I expect my sister made the dresses for very little. I forget what the whole production cost, even if I ever enquired—but the piece was a failure, and we had to take it off after three or four weeks, and put on "Much Ado About Nothing."

Meantime, my work had been heard of in Germany and Germans had come over to London to see it. So when it became obvious to me that E. T. could only carry on with one of her children, I decided to get along to Germany and to Russia and other lands where my notions were regarded without prejudice, and progress was preferred to argumentative retrogression.

But before leaving London I looked around to see if I could note any sign which I could rely on as indicating a desire on someone's part that I should continue to produce more plays.[1] I waited

---

[1] I had already produced in London, in three years, two operas, one ballet and three plays.

and listened and looked around—no one made any sign whatever—so off I went.

Whether my sister got rid of her lunatic assistant, I never enquired. It no longer mattered —she and the foreign fellow and the tame business manager had between them successfully wrecked this venture.

MY dear mother grieved that I was gone, and often she asked me to return and once again do some work with her—but I had realized, through experience, what it would entail. She never found any first-class manager to organize her affairs for her, and her theatrical course, during and after " The Vikings," was zigzag, for she was rudderless.

She could not take and abide by the counsel of any one person, after she left Irving—she had preferred to consult dozens of people about everything, and to annoy them by never entirely following their advice.

For a time she acted, here and there; but of course she was, like all artistes, difficult to manage, and she couldn't work at a loss.

I could, of course, be of no use to E. T. as business director of her theatre: that was not my *métier*. I have never confused the two marked divisions of theatrical work—the stage work and the business work; and it was only the stage work I was concerned with. Selling tickets—buying materials—engaging people—all this and much more is the work of a theatrical expert— it's like selling sweets or motor cars. You can work up either business if you are an expert, until you are a rich man; but it's the game of buying and selling and distributing—and quite a different thing from that of creating. Ibsen, E. T. and I created the work at the Imperial Theatre, but E. T. found no one to sell properly what she and I had made— and made pretty well, I think.

WHEN in 1905 and 1906 my mother Nelly heard of my success in Germany, she was ever so happy . . . passing E. T. by the looking-glass on the stairs, one day, she paused, and they exchanged thoughts.

E. T. simply could not make it out—what did it all mean? "Do you mean to say that Ted (Nelly nodded) has been received with real enthusiasm abroad?" (Nelly nodded three times, rapidly— frightened but smiling) "and that when he was here with us" (a tear sprang out of Nelly's eye and flew across the firmament, and astronomers dis-covered it next night), "when he was here in London, he had started a new art of the theatre?" ("Ummm!"

said Nelly, and nodded five times) " Well, I can't understand it," said E. T., and kissed Nelly Terry affectionately and passed on.

E.T. and Nelly were still two persons in one body—Nelly, who never had a doubt, E. T., who was essentially cautious on most occasions: Nelly wild as nature itself, E. T., attentive to civiliza﹐tion: Nelly, who didn't care a rap whether she had a penny or not, and E. T., careful as anything: Nelly, all impulse and every impulse right as rain, E. T., thinking twice, thrice about things, and even then never quite sure about anything.

This all made up the remarkable personality known as Ellen Terry, who, had she lacked one of her inconsistencies, would have been nothing like the great person she was: but she'd have been just as beautiful a mother.

ELLEN TERRY, THE FAMOUS ACTRESS

I

ELLEN TERRY, the actress, I do not feel myself competent to describe, because she was really rather indescribable: but I can give, in fragments, some suggestions which will help.

I do not write down the things in this book so as to cajole the publics of to-day or of the future into any legend, but to serve as part of my contribution towards a right understanding of the English Theatre of the nineteenth century and after—and, without any futile comparison betwixt this actress and those of the sixteenth and eighteenth centuries, to let it be felt that Ellen Terry was someone who counts very much . . . someone more of value than even many of her enthusiastic adorers quite understood.

FIRST to consider the material Ellen Terry had to work with—her temperament.

It is too easy to say of my mother, Ellen Terry ‹here we can link them together›, that she was wilful, because it is what many have said of her; but I would rather not write of her at all than make her out to be a mild person, or that "touching," "pathetic," "frail" being of the legend—the "lovable Ellen Terry." Of course she was that too, but that was not all.

No mild, yielding, and too reasonable, actress ever counts. Often the wanton and perverse ones are worth more. Rachel and Bernhardt were both wanton and headstrong—nothing could tame the intractable Gabrielli, nor rule the unruly but most dear Sophie Arnould—the passion of the adorable Duse was not to be constrained: assuredly you cannot draw out Leviathan with a hook, neither will she make supplication nor speak soft words to those who try to make a pet of her.

To the end, E.T. had all the impatience of Job; but, like Job, she listened to the voice of God and confessed herself to Him. She died in peace, but towards the end, her days were not so blessed as, we are told, were his.

Yet these impatient ones, since their impatience is ever whirled toward themselves, are to be greatly prized. Mother was so sweet—so good—so resigned —but the glorious, the turbulent Ellen Terry was up in arms all the time—not against what is worth while, but against what she felt, in herself first and in others after, was not worth a fig—and so much is *not* worth a fig.

The merely " lovable " creature of the legend could not have achieved so much as she did: how, then, is this " legend " so firmly associated with her name ?

IT is because, while she did one thing, she preached another. *She* would do as she wished, and ever did so—she would be as rash, as hasty as she liked; it led to something—but to every younger person she preached " forbearance "—they were to be " slow and sure ": " orderliness " and " caution " were to be their watchwords: she wished them all the attributes of a "lovable personality." Hence, folk took *that* to be E.T. She, who lived life, did all she could to prevent girls living their lives—her counsel to them was negative and led to nothing—her own actions positive and led to everything. It wasn't that she did not want them to suffer through experience—it was, strangely enough, that, rightly or wrongly, she really thought that suffering would be not a scrap of use to their small or unbalanced natures.

Hers was a very large and sturdy nature, and curiously well-balanced. She had positive dislikes and prejudices, and was stubborn. She had a big share of concentration and commonsense, and was very rarely led by others. Yet, without going out of her way at all, she liked, if not to hide many of these remarkable qualities, that *they should remain hid* (quite the actress, that), and that but one thing should be felt about her—that she was lovable. What to her did it matter that she should be seen to possess intellect or wits—power—a will? What does it matter to a properly rich person that it be realized that he possesses so much? So it was with her.

But why trouble to hide them? She did not go to any pains to hide qualities which no one suspected she possessed. The world, we must admit, is pretty blind about many excellences. Before the glories of the loveliest architecture, the most perfect music of the world, the majority—including numbers of the cleverest people—are about as non-observant as the celebrated cock was over the jewel.

E.T. soon learnt this, "And," says she to herself, " if my friends want to make me out to be a sweet, gentle, little creature—to suppose me lacking in strength, character, concentration and practical sound sense, let them. Wearing those jewels under my coat is to me just as good as displaying them."

I THINK that Ellen Terry had very little jealousy in her, except of the genuine, old-fashioned kind.

She couldn't be jealous because another actress had acted well, or had been praised by the critics; for, without reckoning herself very highly, she was always sure of herself.

She knew she was not wise, as wisdom goes, nor beautiful, as beauty goes; neither did she suppose herself learned or well-read.

I wonder sometimes what she would have said to Sheridan if she had known him, for she possessed much the same temperament, though she was, I believe, never in debt.

She was extravagant and generous with money, without being a spendthrift, and she couldn't gamble.

She was anything but "hard as a nail in money matters," as Charles Reade wrote in his notebook —if she had been, she would have made money, because she would have left Irving after 1886, and touring the world, would, very easily, have left a small fortune of over £200,000.

For she was a far greater draw than was Charles Wyndham, who left about £197,000, or Bancroft, who left about £174,000—both of whom lived in her time.

They owned theatres, and were directors of theatrical enterprises, and Ellen Terry could not have done that, had she wished to.

L

Ellen Terry comes fourteenth in Mr. John Parker's list of fifty-six celebrated theatrical women testators. First comes Lotta, with £800,000. Sarah Lane is second, with £126,000. Christine Nilsson comes third, with £119,000; Anna Held fourth, with about £71,000; and then Lily Langtry, Mary Shaw, Jenny Lind, Dorothy Donnelly, Mrs. Nye Chart, Ada Rehan, Mrs. Francis H. Burnett, Helen Faucit, and then Ellen Terry.

CHARLES READE calls E. T. " hysterical and sentimental," and unless a woman were some-thing of both, she'd never go on the stage—if she be neither, the stage soon makes her both. What sort of actresses would Duse and Bernhardt have been, had they not been hysterical ? As for being sentimental, " There *are* strings . . . " said Mr. Tappertit.

SHE possessed some powers off the stage which are not often possessed by actors and actresses; for example, she could positively converse. Actors, more often than not, are only able to hold forth: they don't like listening to any reply, or having to answer a question; a string of definite statements—a soliloquy—is their special fancy. They like to fix you down in a chair and make a long speech to you—at you—round you—they seem to want to tie you up in it—and then, having done so, to fix you with one last point. It does not matter whether they speak truth or not—it's their person‹ ality they like to give rein to, and to show off their paces. Then they feel a bit better.

E.T. was never like this—neither was Irving— nor Duse. I believe Bernhardt was inclined to be —but she was far too clever not to break herself of such a trick.

II

THEY say that towards the later part of E. T.'s life—towards the year 1896—her memory be‹ gan to fail. This suggests doddering : I flatly contradict the notion that she ever doddered. Then what was it ?—for she assuredly did forget her words —would click her fingers towards the prompt corner—ask for her line. She even did more—she would write out her part on pieces of paper and pin these up all over the stage—on a window‹ curtain, a chair‹back, a lampshade—anywhere and everywhere. Why?

Because of something inside her which, obstinate and intolerant in her youth, she never quite over‹

came—she couldn't make herself like or tolerate that to which she had taken a dislike.

Ophelia, Beatrice, Portia, Imogen—all these long parts she adored, and, I believe, learnt and retained without difficulty: but when it came to *Pauline* in " The Lady of Lyons," to *Madame Sans-Gêne*, to *Clarice* in " Robespierre "—to mention only a few of the horrors—she loathed them, and that put her in such an obstinate, intolerant mood, that she never could bring herself to learn the lines.[1]

Then she would try to improve matters by re-writing many of the lines: it didn't help very much —she was in revolt against the idiocies of the speeches.

Some actors and actresses have a veneration for the words of the author, and some have not. I think it better to have that veneration than not to. If an actor accepts the play of a serious dramatist, he should abide very faithfully to the text—he should not alter a word without the full approval of the

---

[1] She found the words of " Robespierre " very difficult to retain—she would know them on Saturday and have forgotten them by Monday. As you can see from the speech reproduced here, she marked the words—as road posts in some countries are whitewashed, so that, in the dusk, drivers of carts or motorcars can see them—then she wrote them out.

But *what* a speech ! Lady Alix Egerton tells me that one night in Glasgow, E. T. began the rigmarole thus : " I never had a mother, Mr. Vaughan " . . . but no one laughed—though when she remembered what she had said and how solemnly the audience had taken it, she rocked with joy !

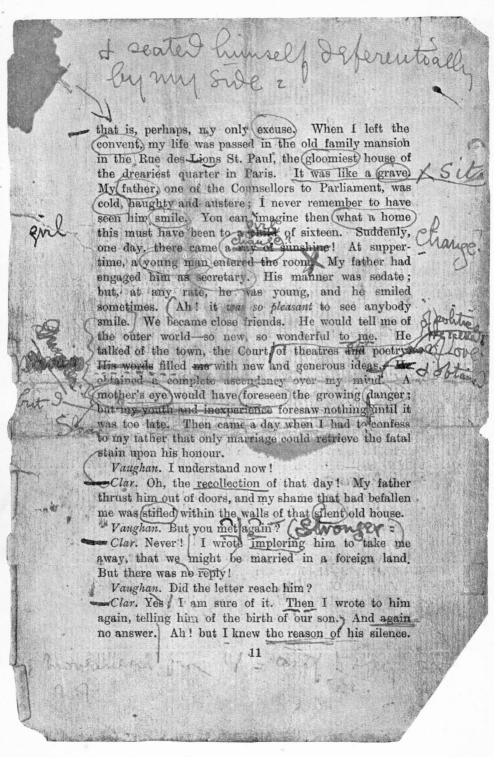

& seated himself deferentially by my side z

that is, perhaps, my only excuse. When I left the convent, my life was passed in the old family mansion in the Rue des Lions St. Paul, the gloomiest house of the dreariest quarter in Paris. It was like a grave. My father, one of the Counsellors to Parliament, was cold, haughty and austere; I never remember to have seen him smile. You can imagine then what a home this must have been to a child of sixteen. Suddenly, one day, there came a ray of sunshine! At supper-time, a young man entered the room. My father had engaged him as secretary. His manner was sedate; but, at any rate, he was young, and he smiled sometimes. Ah! it *was* so *pleasant* to see anybody smile. We became close friends. He would tell me of the outer world—so new, so wonderful to me. He talked of the town, the Court, of theatres and poetry. His words filled me with new and generous ideas. He obtained a complete ascendency over my mind. A mother's eye would have foreseen the growing danger; but my youth and inexperience foresaw nothing until it was too late. Then came a day when I had to confess to my father that only marriage could retrieve the fatal stain upon his honour.

Vaughan. I understand now!

Clar. Oh, the <u>recollection</u> of that day! My father thrust him out of doors, and my shame that had befallen me was stifled within the walls of that silent old house.

Vaughan. But you met again?

Clar. Never! I wrote imploring him to take me away, that we might be married in a foreign land. But there was no reply!

Vaughan. Did the letter reach him?

Clar. Yes, I am sure of it. Then I wrote to him again, telling him of the birth of our son. And again no answer. Ah! but I knew the reason of his silence.

11

girl

sit

change

change

politics interest Love to obtain

change

cut 9 Si

Stronger

PAGE FROM ELLEN TERRY'S BOOK OF STUDY

I never knew my mother
Mr Vaughan . Baby in
arms~ Excuse –
Convent – Life passed –
Family Mansion . Gloomiest
house – like a grave –
Father – Counsellor to P.
was Cold – Smile – Home
for 16 = One day Change
Stranger – Supper – seated
Father – Secretary . Manner
sedate ::: Young – smiled –
pleasant to see Smile –
Close friend . Told me of
Outer World – New & Wonder
ful to me – he talked Town –
Court – Theatres . Poetry . Music
Words filled me New –
generous ideas – Ascendancy
over mind – Mothers Eye person

[See note page 150

PAGE FROM ELLEN TERRY'S BOOK OF STUDY

dramatist. E.T. was given to altering a text—not Shakespeare, but Wills and Sardou, Shaw and Calmour. I have seen in her writing several changes that she made in Wills' " Charles I," and in Shaw's " Captain Brassbound's Conversion," she was always improvising. Of her part in this play, she writes in her book (1908) " My letters to Mr. Shaw were, I suppose, ' good copy,' as he drew the character of *Lady Cicely Waynflete* in ' Brassbound ' entirely from my letters." So honours are easy.

She did not think very much of playwrights— perhaps not half enough—because when she read a play she would for ever find it " halting "—it didn't flow on—it seemed to jerk and . . . in short, was unnatural. It was then that she began to " improve " it—cutting and altering whole sentences.

Tennyson was happy to allow Irving to do this with his " Becket," and it was afterwards printed as Irving had reshaped it. The practice is, I am quite sure, a wrong one . . . but when a great actor breaks the rule, what is to be said ?—evidently there is something to be said, and it is this: that the playwright did not quite know his business

But Irving was quite unconcerned about bad lines—if a play marched, let the damned lines look to themselves, was his comment . . . besides, he had a curious appreciation of those lines which, though bosh, somehow were right and good in their particular place. E.T. draws attention to this when she writes in her book that: "Such lines as *'Tis she ! Her footstep beats upon my heart !*[1] were not absurd from Irving's lips." The reason was that he entered fully into this romantic nonsense, instead of playing the conscientious objector. E. T. had in her more objection to trash than will or cunning to overcome that objection.

III

UNFORTUNATELY E. T. had two masters, a good one and a bad one—the first, Henry Irving, the second, the public.

We hear of the *partnership* of Irving and Ellen Terry, as meaning that both had the same power —it was no such thing. There was only one head of the house, and it was Irving. This house was the Lyceum Theatre, which was head of the English Theatrical world.

E.T., of imagination all compact, fired all the reasonability of life into a blaze; but neither that nor any other blaze could budge Irving from his purpose, to steer a straight course.

She served Irving faithfully, till Shaw began to write her letters to undermine her faith in

[1] " The Corsican Brothers."

Irving (which, by the way, in the end, he failed to do).

Of the public, her other master, she was somewhat frightened. She would be apt to win it round to her by all sorts of compromises which artists have avoided. They have an old law, by which they abide, that the public is not to be considered. Had this law not been obeyed, the world would have had no works of art.

E.T. considered the public, and the public will be happy to have it recorded. Had she been more faithful to herself, and less to them, would she have done better? Perhaps.

This is the only criticism I can make of her as an actress.

She has herself told me what were her faults as an actress—she said: " I always lacked concentration —could not restrain tears—could not easily achieve repose—could not sustain any feeling for very long."

Yet, with all this, she was the best English-speaking actress of her time.

THE English public has always loved to cry if it could get someone to cry with—it will not cry until the actress cries.

The extraordinary thing about my famous mother was that, although she had the capacity to lead the British public—as Irving certainly led them—away from silly sob-stuff, she actually was one of the great sob-stuffers of England.

She had that element in her nature which, for some reason, appeals so to the English—something that is frail, and can be summed up in the two words, " little me." Nothing is more unlike Ellen Terry as I know her to have been. She made the sob-stuff positively classic . . . and that is the worst thing you can do, not the best. If she had made it ridiculous, she would have achieved the very thing she really wanted to do.

Now why was she one of the great sob-stuffers of the age ? For these reasons:

She had a public waiting for her, handkerchief in hand—a tradition by the side of it—and she had wretched plays waiting to be performed, with lines in them, and thoughts and blanks which would give any emotional actor or actress a glorious opportunity to express something vapid.

Bernard Shaw complains of these awful plays,[1] though he seems to encourage the mood, day by day, letter by letter, in his correspondence with E.T.

[1] In 1892, on July 5th, he writes to her of the fearful stuff called "The Amber Heart," which he has had to listen to and watch E. T. playing down to it with all her skill, force and genius. And he tells her that " traitors calling themselves critics " were encouraging her—allowing their brains and consciences to be cajoled away by her beauty.

It is something of the Sidney Carton complex —that Sidney Carton who sweeps through the emotional guts of a nation which has too much mucus in its composition, due to an appalling ignorance which allowed a minority to lay down an eleventh commandment: "Thou shalt suppress all desires."

Ellen Terry plays *Marguerite* in "Faust"; she plays *Olivia;* she plays *Lucy Ashton* in "Ravens⸗wood"; she plays *Iolanthe*—"The Amber Heart": and it will be difficult for the young people of this generation to understand this—that in all these plays she loves to "make them all cry," and begins to cry in order to do it.

Duse loved to do the same thing: in one of her letters from South America, she shows how delighted she is to drown her audience in its own tears.

"The first night was 'Fédora'," she writes. "The audience was cold, and the performance a complete fiasco. It was an immense Theatre ; I felt weak and small in it, and it seemed impossible for me to throw my voice to the back of the pit. I was obliged to say 'I love you' to *Loris*, as I might have said 'Get away,' in order to make my voice carry far enough.

"A continuous worrying murmur of conversation was kept up in the stalls and boxes until the end of the play ; my head and my voice were tired out ; I changed my dress as fast as possible, and hurried home, locking myself in my room. What sadness, what a void I felt after that evening. . . . The next day the papers gave no criticism of the perfor‹ mance at all, and merely said that I had a certain something about me, 'non so che,' that had made an impression on the audience, but that of my words, apart from the difficulty of the language (my soft Italian and their hard Portuguese and their still harder Brazilian) they had heard but barely half.

"The second performance was 'Denise'. The Theatre, that huge place, half empty; four or five rows of stalls and four or five boxes, those nearest the stage, were occupied, partly by press; and here there was little attention. My poor *Denise*, simple, without fine costume, without rank, with no resem‹ blance to that feverish *Fédora*, compelled attention.

"In the first and second acts I cried, and in the third act I made them cry, as much as I would, and as much as I could."

But there are a few other purposes in the Dramatic art, and one of these is to fire your audiences. Rachel and Sarah Siddons knew this, and Bernhardt knew it too: Kean knew it and Irving knew it . . . though after seeing him once as *Charles I*, when my mother played *Henrietta Maria* with him, I in future avoided that play.

But it was quite other with the English public of that day: it loved " a good cry " . . . I am told there is a large section of that public that still loves a good cry—and likes it best very soppy, and to last very long.

How my mother used to laugh when anybody was like that—what astounding virility and power in her healthy sense of humour ! And yet, *faced with the public*, rather than carry the public along, or fight it, she would side with the cow-like animal and begin to imitate its face and to drop tears all over the place.

Now why did she give in about this ? She was even pathetic as *Lady Macbeth*.

If there was ever anybody born in nineteenth century England to give a real and painful inter-pretation of *Lady Macbeth* it was Ellen Terry, if only she had not been frightened of that British public. There she was, with the heritage of Mrs. Siddons waiting for her, if she would only take it up. What made Mrs. Siddons seem, even to Byron, greater than Kean ? . . . it was her ascendancy over the public—she refused to be dominated by it, and made tearful by it when she was about to scorch and brand it.

It is this which places Mrs. Siddons at the head of the theatrical profession; and any other actor or actress who wishes to don her cloak must first do as she did—dominate the public. Rachel did so in France, the moment she stepped on the stage. Mrs. Siddons, having the advantage of the English text of Shakespeare, has the advantage of

Rachel and everybody. And although even in her day the English public was being brought up by that old ass Bowdler to sniff at Shakespeare's "horrible and disgusting notions," when Siddons said "Come to my woman's breasts and take my milk for gall!" the English public still honoured the poet and the actress by shuddering.

By the time Ellen Terry came to say it, Shake‚ speare was no more liked—anything but loved—and held as a bit of a highbrow: so E.T. felt she had to take care—and one heard her saying under her breath to the British public: "Now, my dear, dear people, you won't *really* think I am a horrid woman like that, will you?"

Now that won't do—that is capitulation.

Then, in the sleep‚walking scene, you did not shudder at the thought beneath the words: "The Thane of Fife had a wife—where is she now?" You only felt: "Poor Ellen Terry—she is so sorry for the Thane of Fife's wife, and is wondering where she can possibly be now, poor, poor dear. What a *nice* woman!"[1]

---

[1] Before she undertook the part of *Lady Macbeth*, articles appeared in the papers, stating that *Lady Macbeth* was not as she had been hitherto represented, but was a most loving, gentle wife—essentially feminine meaning by that something mild) who did her best to keep *Macbeth* straight, and the failure to do so utterly wrecked her, and she died.

In almost every play then being written, the leading lady was one who kept the hero straight—it was of no use to point out that this notion was in contradiction to nature : the work of Calvin, Wesley, Bowdler,

So then, it was more the fault of the public than that of Ellen Terry, for, as all her true friends will tell you, she had, by the grace of God, a bit of a demon in her,[1] which the whole world knows to be just what is wanted by the creative or interpretative artist. No, it was the public's fault—and the fault of that large group of private publicists, always to the fore, and for ever stating what is right, what is wrong, what is art and what isn't, what we all *must* do and mustn't: this group takes precedence of the nation itself, and betrays the nation, year in and year out. Now I may only be in a majority of ten million, but I hold that we should be strong enough to prevent that public betraying our nation.

Ellen Terry saw it from another point of view. To her, this public *was* the nation—though how four thousand people can be the nation, is more than I can say. In 1881, the time of which I write, the population of London was 3,816,483, and the theatre going public numbered about 200,000— i.e., a nineteenth part of the London public.

---

had borne fruit, and we were in for a period of fraudulent writers, artists and actors, who would echo the humbug—for it paid so well to pass it along to the public.

The fraud could be successfully handled in England—the reason given being its insularity—what a feather in the cap of the Irish that, though insular too, their artists have ever fought for and preserved for their public so much that is everlastingly worth while.

[1] Just a *bit*.

Although perhaps about one-third of the whole nation had heard of Ellen Terry, and had heard the legend about her, many more than twenty-five millions of them would never have seen her.

Now Mr. Bernard Shaw has very rightly stated that this small section of the nation was a ghastly kind of public, and had as its advisers a treacherous pack of critics, which could love Ellen Terry for her faults and utterly waste her magnificent possibilities—and that she *was* wasted is to be seen by going through the repertory and noting that when she was at her best, she was least popular. Her despairing cry is, over and over again, " What is the good of acting something in which they won't come and see me ? "

But what did this clever man propose, in his letters to her ?

He positively suggested that she should play for a still smaller public—a public which read advanced books, without understanding them, and disliked the Theatre at its best. It must be said for this advanced public that it certainly disliked the Theatre at its worst, and it hated sentimentality; but it had inherited the curse laid on it by the puritans and their prejudice against that which we call the beautiful.

This public, which was already in England before the 19th century, was no good for Ellen Terry. That this puritanical group has to some extent braced up the sob-stuff public is not difficult to realize; but that it can, in the phrase of Walt Whitman, "filtre and fibre its blood," is quite another matter: it is very doubtful if it will affect its blood in the very least.

People at a serious English theatre become like awkward boys at school, who want to get away and play football. That's a bad state to have got a serious public into. After some years of this, they say, "Yes, it's very good indeed, very clever—but no more—for goodness' sake, no more!" and then they keep away from the Theatre altogether. If it is a question of having to cry their eyes out or to rack their brains, they would far sooner get away to the football match and feel comfortable and jolly—and I am with them entirely.

III

ELLEN TERRY went to no school of Dramatic Art. Her father and mother were acting when she was born, now in one town, now in another; and her elder sister Kate was already a beginner on the stage: and E. T. writes in her memoirs that "in those days theatrical folk did not imagine that their children *could* do anything but follow their parents' profession."

So then like the duckling, who follows the duck and drake into the water without any tuition at all, and swims like a duck, Ellen Terry followed her father and mother and sister onto the boards, and acted at once like an actress.

Instinctively she did everything in the right way.

But "a good poet's made as well as born," writes Ben Jonson—which proves that a good poet is something different from a good duck.

And now the questions begin—

Does the actor resemble most the duck or the poet? The actor is compared too often with the poet, the painter, the musician—with I know not what extraordinary *reasoning* people—seldom with the instinctive animals.

The dancer is compared with the musician and the poet, and not with the lamb who gambols, nor with the bird—nor with the bareback-rider or the equilibrist.

There is much confusion in the minds of people as to who exactly is an artist and who is not—what constitutes an art and what does not: and the result of this confusion of mind has been to create a confused lot of fraudulent rubbish which an easily-fuddled world calls works of art, because they are labelled so by dealers.

This has tended to bring the genuine arts into disrepute, to the impoverishment of our daily life.

I will not discuss here the question whether or no acting is an art, for I have dealt with that in my other books: what I am concerned with here is one particular actress, and it will not forward us to stop and reconsider in detail all the pros and cons, nor the several theories about acting—but these few words had to be jotted down.

ELLEN TERRY was a born actress, and each new piece of work—I would say each perfor⸗ mance—was a new birth. Her performances were not *made*, in the same sense as Irving's were. Her acting was the exact antithesis of his—spontaneous, genial, free.

I wrote in my book on Irving that Ellen Terry was very much a daughter of Shakespeare, and when she spoke his prose it was as though she but repeated something she had heard at home—some⸗ thing said that morning. It seemed the easiest thing in the world to do, and the unskilful supposed it as easy as it seemed, and that being easy, it could not be acting—it must be what is called " natural."

M

I must avoid going into all that here, and will content myself by saying that whenever we use the human body as an instrument—be it to sing, to dance or to act—it is generally conceded that it is preferable for that body to seem natural, rather than unnatural. Whatever " art " *Romeo* or *Juliet* may exercise as they come before us, we like them best when they reveal to us that one touch of nature which makes the whole theatrical world kin.

" *One* touch of nature "—it is an interesting point to consider how many touches of nature an actor can safely give in the course of a scene, without spoiling all he has done with that inimitable first touch. And Ellen Terry did consider this, and carefully, or certain touches would not live in our memory as they do . . . for example, the unfor׳ gettable action at the end of the trial scene of " The Merchant of Venice," when *Bassanio* refuses to part with the ring.

E. T. drew us all together, silently, immediately : that to begin with. And I do not think it was because she was a woman. I think it was because she was an Irishman. Had Sheridan been an actor, that is what he would have done—drawn the five thousand spectators all together and made them one.

While Irving was so still—seldom moving—she was all movement.

With Irving it was, above all, his face which commanded—for when, as in *Othello*, *Lear* and *Coriolanus*, his face was black or bearded, something of his power was gone.

With Ellen Terry it was the whole person; even with her head in a bag, she would have captured the house. Tie her hands and ankles, and it would have been harder. So it would seem as though much lay, with her, in her movement—and indeed, an entrance with her, was a gliding, eager thing. She was very rapid in her light, long strides—large in her gestures— measured in her delivery—and impossible to follow in the variety of her expression.

She did not depend much on bits of business, as we call them; her power lay in entering any character and making herself one with it—" getting under the skin of a part " is the phrase used by the profession.

And it came to be said of her that she possessed in the very highest degree the art which conceals art. The good actress will ever strive to cover up all traces of how she makes her effects—and the best way to do this is not to make effects, lest the spectator should fancy he is witnessing a display of Brock's fireworks.

To come on without effect—to slip onto the stage—to be there without showing how she got there—that would be Ellen Terry's aim.

This makes it clear that she was not by choice a melodramatic actress—the melodramatic is, I think, essentially a masculine affair.

She was not startling—her effects were broad (she was never niggling) but broad, not big. She spread herself, and encompassed the stage, the stalls, the pit, gallery, and somehow the air—she mingled with these, came out—always out—to them. An immense reserve, not of power but of gifts, seemed to be moving with her—never at any moment did we expect her to overwhelm us with the thunders and lightnings of rhetoric, but always with *largesse*.

E.T. was a scatter-heart. To right and to left she threw her heart's thoughts as she came onto a stage, for she was rich in heart—prodigal of it: the more she gave, the more she had—in this she was one of the wisest among wise women. But remember, lest you mistake me—it is of her heart I speak.

It was, I think, the most compassionate thing in our land. Such a heart cannot be " pathetic "— " touching "—" frail," for the reason that these minor littlenesses are lost in so large a thing.

Do you never came up to Kensington now? — I took a rather long walk this morning from Turner's house on the Embankment all down & around to Westminster — I wore very thick boots & went quite alone — the river was lovely, & I thought of you (& its turkey! —) & Wordsworth. & Edward — — — & Jimmy Whistler — & Henry & Joy! & of my boy Ted, & Edy, & I was mighty happy & not tired at the time! but — now!!! well, I think Bed is the only place for me for it is just ten o'clock, & a nice fire in my room draws me off to sleep — Good night dearest Dear — Your old old friend Nelana =

Tomorrow I'm off to Essex — to stay a week with Edie Goynne (Jane.)

A PAGE FROM A LETTER
FROM E.T. TO MR. GRAHAM ROBERTSON
(27th December, 1917)

"I am not clever—I'm a Fool," she wrote me (1918–19): "for being all heart?" we may ask her, and leave it at that.

That certainly is a risk—it is the risk that *Cordelia* and *Ophelia* took, and *Imogen*.

I had hesitated to speak of these beings, lest their names should signify nothing in 1931. They certainly seem to have vanished from our world— gone away suddenly. Were you to ask an acquaintance, "Have you seen *Imogen* lately?" it is possible that the reply would be, "No—but I saw Lady Mancatous only yesterday." So *Imogen* is dead and gone, and no one need be sorry for her. Perfectly splendid—*she's* away—*she's* out of it—hurrah for death, and glory to those who are lost.

IV

DID Shakespeare create any objectionable "strong-minded" women? I can find none. But I find women of power—not the petty power to be a cat, but the power to refrain from that thing. When he drew the terribly weak characters like *Goneril*, *Regan*, or *Lady Macbeth*, he was again on his favourite theme—madness. But the majority of his characters are sane—of

good health—of fine appearance—and their particular
quality is power.

Ellen Terry was able to depict such power, because
she was able to enter into such existences easily.
The strange hallucinations of *Lady Macbeth*
puzzled her too much; had she attempted *Goneril*,
she would have despaired. Every actor or actress
has limitations, and most of the actresses find
Portia, Beatrice, Imogen, and *Cordelia* quite beyond
their range. These actresses, clever though they
may be, are altogether too slight—they cannot
fill out such grandeur. Cleverness alone cannot
cope with either a *Beatrice* or an *Imogen*. To
put on airs—to play the fine lady—is not enough
when it comes to bringing *Portia, Cordelia,
Hermione* or *Queen Katharine* to life—I think
you must have power.

Ellen Terry had it, for it was in these very parts
she shone.

She played her many selves in playing the Shakespearean heroines, and only now and then was she
obliged to play anything at all weak, for most of the
heroines in Shakespeare are remarkable for
their strength. Only a very few of them are at
all worldly—only a rare few are rather stupid—
and not one of them is merely sweet or sentimental
or comfortable.

BEFORE I saw her as *Beatrice, Portia, Mistress Page*, I had never stopped to think what these people, *Beatrice, Portia* and *Mistress Page* might be like: the moment I saw her, I understood.

I had read the plays—but I'm afraid it is true that male actors do not stop much to consider who these women are.

Beatrice was always poking fun—I could see that—and became furious when her cousin *Hero* was slandered—good girl, *Beatrice*, quite the right sort. *Portia* had a fan—because I'd seen pictures of her with a fan and a black boy as attendant—she was giving the little black a key: and I knew that she, too, was the right sort, because at the end of the play she dressed up as a man and went all the way from Belmont to Venice to stick up for a Christian man who had got himself into a muddle over an unfair contract with a distinguished Jewish gentleman.

That's all I knew about these two of the four ladies, when I was younger: and when I saw them —saw and heard them—at once, in a flash, I understood that these people were all my mother; and it went without saying that they were real people —capable of everything that was wonderful, nice, beautiful to see, exciting, and that they would make me laugh in a moment—and before the very next one, they had done so.

"Got him!" I cried to myself—the great thing at school was to catch the other fellow, and my whole notion of a heroine of Shakespeare was her ability to get the other fellow's goat.

Later on, when I saw *Mistress Page*, I knew something more about her: but not so very much, I discovered, as the curtain of His Majesty's went up on that immortal first night, and before long E. T. came on, reading a letter from *Falstaff*, and revealing the obvious.

"That is how to act comedy," was all one could nod—and I nodded and nodded, and was terribly excited to see not only the ease of the actress, but to receive an entirely successful explanation of what it was all about. *All* about—one had it all—and all at once, but one never knew how it was done. It was revelation—one knew what was coming—a feast. All one wanted to do was to sit back and let it go on for ever and ever.

And that is not what we get as a rule—we get a nibble here, and there a bite, and a little milk to wash it down with—and a nice round of applause at the end of the act.

Here it was a banquet. Boar's head, miraculous stuffed peacock, fountains of wine and Shakespeare seemed to be standing in the wings, cooking; and the incredible part of the whole evening was that we, the audience, all seemed for once to have huge appetites.

There was Tree—famous—admirable—light as froth: there Madge Kendal, exquisite and inimitable and entrancingly beautiful—and here was E. T. reading a letter, and making the words bubble and glow as though she had but read them to herself that very moment.

"Ask me no reason why I love you," she began —and the whole audience responded, "We don't"; and at the end of it, without reason, told her how they loved her.

"The way to do it," was the verdict when the curtain came down.

BUT with *Ophelia* it was quite another matter. I saw her play this after 1906—anyhow, when she was rather older—but I was older too.

I had not only played *Hamlet* but I had been giving some years of careful study to the whole play, and had come to some very serious conclusions about *Ophelia*. My book was scored with notes, plans, suggestions of all kinds, and indeed I knew my *Ophelia* pretty well.

So I was quite differently interested when I came to Drury Lane one day—came over from Berlin—I forget what the occasion was—a big benefit, I think: at any rate, I was in London—it was a sunny afternoon—and everyone was at Drury Lane; and so I popped in at the stage door to see what was on. I knew E. T. was to do *Ophelia's* mad scene—and for the last time in her life—and I thought I would compare my own notions with her performance.

I got down to the prompt corner, just in time . . . and on came E. T.

Well, the rest of the story is told, for there is no more to tell.

The whole of my fabric was rent and consumed, like the fabric in a dream. I could not compare my notions with hers, because mine were all scattered and she hadn't any—she had no notions—she was the thing itself.

All was faultless—and all I could do was to look and listen and look again, and murmur in between times a prayer for forgiveness.

This was revelation—more powerful and far more beautiful than on that first night of *Mistress Page*. When the curtain came down, the thought left with us was not "That's the way to do it," but "It is the only way to do it."

SHE AGES AND DIES

I

NELLY TERRY liked nice-looking houses, but her fancy was always towards a cottage. Life to her was always growing more and more real, and to her it was not made a scrap more real by luxury. She would prefer a small, plain, rather hard bed to a big one—white walls to those covered by tapestry or beautifully designed wallpapers—plain tables and chairs gave her more sense of reality than any others. Periods in furniture did not appeal to her—a good piece of furniture she liked, if it had a real look—but she did not collect wildly. The plainest dresses were the ones she loved best to put on, but though plain, they never had any austere touches—all things had to be real and human, for her to like them. Linen she loved—white or blue—when washed and re-washed and becoming soft and pliable, the coarsest linen often pleased her best. Silks—oh yes—but not like perfect linen. Furs—one, maybe, in a blue moon, but I hardly think she cared for one. Lace—very much she liked to touch and wear lace—but not if too wonderfully costly and rare.

A pony-trap, if not a swell one, delighted her—she drove well—but a motor-car she was not much attracted to. In her pony-trap she could drive herself down some lane and there discover a cottage, and the discovery was more real to her, more really wonderful, than if come at in any other way.

She laughed a little at motor-cars and their fuss of machineries, which so easily went wrong, kicked up such a rumpus, and took so long to adjust. In a moment, a cart and horse were adjusted.

I AM writing still of Nelly—Nelly, grown older and outliving E. T., was just the same as she always was—just as real. Theatre not forgotten, but as a page turned over and read—she could easily turn back and glance at it again—and be reminded of it all.

Stage-struck she ever was, just as she was always moon-struck. Her talk to me was very often of the moon and what it meant to her: she could not define it—she was just a little moon-struck, and there it was.

And the moon comes into many, many of her letters—not only to me, but to others. She seemed to be able to resolve doubts and difficulties after two hours' quiet in the garden, when all the Farm was asleep, at Smallhythe—or in the Winchelsea

garden—maybe, too, at Harpenden, in her earlier
years. The sun did not play the same part one
could have supposed it might play in such a tempera⁄
ment . . . for her it was always the moon which
meant so much.

I am reminded for a moment of a sheet of paper
on which Eleonora Duse once wrote me a stage
direction. I was to design her some scenes for
"Rosmersholm," and I asked her to write down
for my guidance some point about each scene, as
she saw it: and on coming to the last scene, she
wrote, in her immense calligraphy:

"*La Lune—la lune—la lune !—Folie—amour—
mort——*"

I am reminded of this, and of Duse as she wrote,
and of the reality to her of this same moon; and I
put down this remembrance here because it is no
more, but no less, indicative of something I would
say and cannot express about Nelly Terry, even as
the words were a guide to me about my scene.

Anything less practical one could not suppose—
nor anything more indicative. But one has to come
at it without reasoning about it and so I beg of
you to do, for plenty of people there are to smile
at an Eleonora or a Nelly who is moon⁄struck
. . . even a few will dare to frown and take steps.

BUT much as Nelly, my mother, was taken by the moon, and however much she would write about that strange sphere, so powerful in its influences, believe me she could write and talk quite as well about apples and turnips . . . and relatively enjoy them as much.

She was particularly fond of turnips, when mashed up and after she had added a little butter and pepper and salt: and she would write down most practically how many turnips were to be bought at the market, and how many potatoes too, and how much was to be paid for them—and what was the exact kind of apple to bring back.

She was as real about moon and turnip as she was about art and life. Eleonora Duse, I feel, ran her close in sound commonsense, but I think even she lacked some of E. T.'s executive power. When it came to cooking—washing children—ordering dinner—and thinking of what would please others to eat, to wear, to look at and to listen to—there I *think* E. T. (with the aid of Nelly) beat Eleonora hollow.

But of that I am not quite sure, for geniuses are such surprising people.

I have found that the genius can generally do so very many things better than anybody else, and I have rarely found an exception to this rule.

I will take E. T. as an illustration. She could, when past seventy, really drive an old cart and pony down difficult paths until past ten at night, and the ways quite dark—when other people would be fussing and talking about the risk, and so on. She never had an accident—she took all the care that genius does take.

It will surprise many people, and tax their credulity a little, to believe that genius does take care . . . it takes infinite care.

E. T. even took care to reply to the sixty plaintive requests for help or sympathy which she would receive weekly. Duse would not have to take such care, for Italian ladies are not brought up to be quite so sorry for themselves as were those who wrote to E. T., whose post would bring in one wail after another, to most of which she lent an attentive ear and a helping hand.

I suppose one would imagine that genius could not lay a table . . . she could do it better and more rapidly than anybody I know. The secrets of the craft of making a bed were all known to her —and I know one or two of these secrets that are still unknown to some of the best housemaids of the best hotels in Europe.

Oh, she could cook an apple tart! and make the crust delicious; and I think that Escoffier himself could not make a salad better than she.

But in matters of the table I am forgetting all about the wonders—quite simple wonders—which she could, *when she wished,* produce.

For that was the whole thing with her—*when she wished* . . . and genius has a queer faculty of knowing when to do a thing and when not, where to do it and where not. I am afraid that this often appears to other people to resolve itself into a much pettier " When I please," and of course that is, in a sense, quite inexcusable. Yet " When I please " is always meant by the man or woman of genius to stand for " When I can "—you remember that line on the frame of the Jan Van Eyck picture in the National Gallery "As I can." Hectoring folk will always hold that the man who is about to write the "Iliad" or design the Forth Bridge, must do it to suit everybody else. But we hold that he must do it at the time when he knows that he can do it, and in the way that suits him, and at no other time and in no other way . . . for if everything else does not fit in with him, the "Iliad" will never be written, the bridge never designed.

That, of course, is the one weak point about genius. Could a few of the practical men write the "Iliad" better, do you think ?—could they do it sitting round a noisy printing machine in Fleet Street, or listening to a whole street full of squalling urchins, or where the insistent gramophone may start its song at any moment, a barrel-organ follow on, and a choice stream of chortle-horns disturb what is left of the silence?

Anyhow, the director of the Lyceum Theatre held other views about the condition necessary to do good work. In all theatres, the performers are obliged to arrive, and be ready, by the time the curtain goes up—they have no say in that matter—and of course at the Lyceum it was the same. But at the Lyceum there was the same silence on the stage, at rehearsals and during the performance, as there was in that very disciplined theatre, the Deutsches Theater, when Reinhardt directed it . . . though I think perhaps I was never aware of quite such a silence as was observed on his stage.

Now why this silence, unless it is that the thing called genius is being really respected? Such a silence cannot be produced by people merely keeping passive and orderly through indifference. It has to be an intense and active silence, for it to be remarked.

I have touched on this because the general impression is that genius is a happy-go-lucky sort of a thing, undisciplined, thoughtless, careless, and

N

this is the opinion which obtains very generally in England—far too generally.

REPLYING to her correspondence was rather a tax on E. T.'s time and generosity, and so, as time went on, she was assisted by one secretary after another. Girls who admired her would work for her on her correspondence, on the house, on anything which came to hand, all for love of E. T. . . . but strangely enough, some of these helpful girls gave her more trouble than did the plaintive ones writing to her for a little help.

It's hardly to be supposed, but some of these young ladies were " terrors." She has written to me of that, and it has puzzled me not in the least —for it is almost a speciality of disciples or assistants who work for love of anything, to grow more critical than a man's valet, or a lady's maid.

The fact is that E. T. was just as " difficult " as any other artist : practical—too practical—she could, as I have suggested, generally beat most people hollow at doing anything. But you can't do a hundred things a day—and when it's your duty, you are generally provided with first-class executants who carry out what has to be seen to, and save you trouble. That's the notion—the idea—the thing that we are told happens.

Whereas it's something of a delusion. These assistants are seldom trained sufficiently well, and are for ever fancying that they know so much better than those whom they are assisting—and when their very masters do not in time come to do as they are told, the assistants become positively abusive.

E.T., up to a certain time in her life, always had her own way—thought and said rapidly what first came to mind, and did as she wished.

But there came a time when others liked to direct her, and then it was that, being preoccupied and a little too tired to bother about where she went or what she did, she, many a little time, let herself be pushed here and there—allowed herself to be made to do this or that.

Then it was that, rather than quarrel with these pushing people, she would tell herself that her time was gone; and since she had already done enough to show what mettle she was made of, what did it matter to her? She had seen and heard enough, too—and would sit a while longer, and remember it all.

If all the women around her at that time could have done a particle of what Ellen Terry had done and could do, it would not have been so bad, and there would have been no need for those many books which came out then setting down what the Intelligent Woman *should* do, and how she *might* do it. These books were written for several kinds of women—not for Ellen Terry.

In October, 1906, I received a letter from her, saying:

"Yesterday I went to the River in a motor and then *on* the river—with a very nice man[1] —I am so sick of being eternally with crowds of women—they just *bore* me—and always want something being done for them."

There had been a time in Ellen Terry's life when, for some unknown reason, she thought she preferred the society of women to that of men, or of men and women together. Why? Well, she took them to be sisters of *Imogen*, *Portia*, *Ophelia*. She thought that they must be wonderful—since Shakespeare had drawn his characters from the English stock . . . she confused reality and the dream of the artist: so at that time, one could never see her but she would have round her some women. If one managed to draw her away from these kindly creatures (one she likens to a wild tiger in disguise) and get away with her to some restaurant, and eat a little and talk a lot, it was a rare chance,

[1] I think this must refer to Mr. James Carew.

a great delight, and she seemed to enjoy every moment of it: but it was a delight which was soon to end—for sure enough, one or more of the dozen demoiselles would turn up and carry her off.

I remember that I seldom saw her out at lunch or driving with her old and valued men friends—though one or another would occasionally manage to tease her into going here and there . . . perhaps she was more easily persuaded into going to a theatre than anywhere else, for then she recovered herself and her old spirits, through contact with the theatre public. But I never saw or heard of her being taken out anywhere by Mr. Bernard Shaw and it seems to me this could have made her so happy for an hour . . . . . and now and again.

" Tie up the knocker, say I'm sick, I'm dead."

E. T. was ever prone, from her youth, to take refuge in the Victorian excuse, "not very well." As she grew in years—indeed, as early as 1900—this habit of hers increased alarmingly. . . . " Poor Ellen Terry, she's so ill," everyone would be saying—when really she was ever so well. She preferred this excuse to another, because she knew it absolved her from hurting people's feelings. To people she'd like to see, but *somehow* felt she didn't want to see at that moment, "Am *quite* TOO ILL to see a *soul*," she'd write—and she was in actuality pretty fit. "X came to see me Monday, and Q came to-day, but I was too ill to be very glad to see anyone," merely meant, if she was very fond of them, that she was terrified lest she had not been up to the mark, and been a drag on them. Later, when X and Q met, and retold each of his day with E.T., it would be one shout of joy and one burst of laughter after another, retelling each incident of the day— how gay and terrifically herself she had been. Never anyone was actually less ill than she.

Through the letters to G.B.S., the excuse, "too ill for words," pops up incessantly.

I remember being in Brindisi or some port with her, on board a P. & O. Liner. She was invited by friends to go on land and dine—it had been arranged before she left England, I gathered—but suddenly she began to show those familiar signs of revolt— and then I knew that ere long she would be saying how *ill* she felt; and sure enough, she did. Then, when the delightful people arrived, she did some fine acting of one who, though ill, makes a real effort . . . but all unavailing. So they went away: and she at once wrote home to a friend of theirs in London how *beautifully dressed* one was—how *delightful* another was—and so on: and doubtless the information came round at last to Brindisi, that being where she wanted it to come, *lest she had seemed rude*—to make all good once more.

The social life did not amuse her. The hurried meetings—the curious and the bores . . . the luncheons and suppers which a few rare clever women arrange and do so well, she seldom bothered about at any time.

I recall writing to her in her last years (when she seemed to me very fit, and I knew she was well-to-do) trying to persuade her to spend more money—to take a better house than the rather cramping little flat she had at Burleigh Mansions, and to hold a little bit of an intellectual and friendly Court. Yes, a little Court—for after all, she was Ellen Terry, Queen of the English stage—and I felt the flat was not enough for her.

I fancied her in the evenings—if only once a week—seated at the head of her table, candles in branched silver candelabra, with eight or ten guests, men of mark—artists—travellers—scientists . . . but no, she wouldn't do it. And whenever I was able to see her, it was only among ladies—a rare few of them very delightful, and for whom she had a real affection: the delightful ladies were ever buoyant and refreshing wherever they appeared— and it was this she needed, and too seldom got.

Other women, less delightful and very jealous, were apt to exhaust her, and, without meaning to do so, positively preyed upon her. A few of these women even wished to control everything she did, and for a number of years, alas, she was surrounded by those who tussled over her, pulling her this way or that way, to her despair.

Always prone to see the humorous side of things, she laughed herself to death at this fine impertinence. Fifteen years previously, she had laughed to see how amusingly Mr. Bernard Shaw wished to direct her powers into better channels than those they had instinctively flowed into—the great Shakespearean stream, with Irving guiding the boat.

It has to be admitted that after Irving's death she was rather naughty, in that she had a way of *seeming* to ask for direction; because, after having asked for it and got it, she seldom took it. This pathetic prelude, lasting days or even weeks—sometimes even years—always preceded a hearty burst of laughter; and it was always, like so many musical preludes, touching, charming, weak, like something advancing into the unknown—plaintive and *adagio* . . . to be followed, as a musical prelude generally is, by an *allegro*.

But it was not done with sly intent, this coaxing way—it was but one more example of that undying eagerness—her hope, spite of all the experience of fifty years, that she would see one more glimpse of a lovely humanity. This hope would express itself in a pause—listening, looking, standing—unresisting and inexpressive—before the new year, the new week or day—tuned to seize the very faintest messages —tuned up at last to breaking-pitch—when the strings snap.

So it is with the poets and the great men—and she was sister to them.

In my mother's nature there was always that immense hope that great revelations were about to be made to her: and that is why she responded so sensitively to the faintest answers which she received to her eternal question.

So it is with all such natures as hers: and these are the very natures which the sententious and incapable invariably believe to be the slightly faulty natures—rather feeble natures—natures which need picking up. You often hear such people being told to "pull themselves together." At the end of her life, Ellen Terry—you would hardly believe it—was often told to pull herself together.

Although very positive when she acted (I don't mean on the stage, I mean in her life) she was curiously hesitant before she could bring herself to decisions: and it was for the reason I have given.

II

IT was because she loved, really loved so well all things both great and small, that she was what she was. Some rare few natures there are here and there who to-day give out such love. The hearts and minds of men and women (some who read this) roughened by bitterest experience, yet longing to feel once more kind towards those to whom they now bear a grudge or two, may find no love to give, and so may grow ever harder and harder.

Towards the end of her life, even E.T. may seem to have grown a *little* harder: but I have seen her whole heart's love well out as it must have done at twenty—and seen her light up with her full force of beauty—once in 1927, when, stricken with ill-health and crouching under a sense of fear and distrust, maybe, she had begun to draw back into her shell more and more.

She had asked me a question—I answered her. . . . How she sprang up!—lash! went her arm around my neck—she became twenty-three—such a kiss!—and subsided again and became seventy-nine again.

I have been told that during the last years she became, as old people are apt to be, a little trying to those around her—that she wanted to govern things as once she did, and could not—or would not—or was not allowed to.

Much was taken from her—she was told she was not well enough to do this or that—quite often told that, I understand.

I speak mainly after re·reading the letters she wrote me, because during her last years I lived in Italy, and three or four people had the looking after of her affairs—her house and her person. They moved her from her old house in Chelsea, sold many of her belongings—amongst them some of the presents I had given her—some drawings of mine and rare copies of "The Page" (I know the people who bought them)[1]—and moved her to a not very Terry·like flat in St. Martin's Lane.

She aged rather considerably here, and sometimes struck me as being rather frightened. I remember when I came over in 1927 on a telegraphic call from London which said she was seriously ill, I

[1]*A letter written by her to me on the day of the sale runs :—*
" 215, King's Road, Chelsea
(*This address struck out with her pen and after it*) :
" Gone ! Sale today and I away—laid up in Port.

" Of course I bought the book *at once*—(*This was 'The Theatre Advancing'*) and of course I sit up in the quiet nights and read it until my eyes begin to drop out . . . . ."

I insert this bit of her letter lest anyone should suppose that she herself would sell one of my gifts or knowingly permit the sale.

found her pretending to be far more ill than she would in secret allow she was. Few people were allowed to see her. All she needed was her free, dom and the free passage to her of all those who cared to see her realize her old self. This old self was just a little crestfallen . . . but under this I saw lots of good rebellion, and good acting; for after all, she was Ellen Terry, and with Ellen Terry the actress was always uppermost. She would act every part she took a fancy to in her room, and deceive those whom she could deceive.

So now she acted the part of one who forgets the names of everyone—at times the highest comedy, it now and again became a little tragic in her hands.

Now she would act someone who is being perse, cuted, and would pretend that some woman had struck her.

" Am I an old hag, Ted ? " she asked me; and when I said I had never seen that impersonation of hers, she smiled and said: " Dear Dash says I am."

How pathetic that was ! Now she would follow this up by a marvellous pretence at such downright fear, that she would make me promise not to say one word—for her sake—lest she should suffer more.

I would have tried to release her from this paradise, but I knew it was useless—it would have meant dragging her into pieces.

Once when I was in the sitting-room, I remember her, swathed in bed-clouts, come hastily in, closing the door, looking back and forwards, and finally coming appealingly to me for help against some thing known or unknown, with a name or without one. She exhibited all the signs of fear, yet could not define one. It left me with an impression that the roof, floors, staircase, doors, furniture, and every person in the house, were in some way preparing to do her harm.

I was about to ask her what it was I could do, and had started to inspect the house, when she drew me back into the room again—put her finger on her lips, whispering a long and tragic " *Shhhh* "— slipped out of the room, closing the door very quietly . . . and that's all I could ever make of it. For after a discreet delay of five minutes I went away, and meeting someone in the passage, was asked if I would post a letter when I went out.

I HAVE no doubt that these incidents would be explained by a number of people to totally different conclusions. I am not in the least interested in explanations—least of all in those which damage E.T. or E.T.'s friends, those friends who wanted nothing from her . . . a rare few.

What interests me in this incident is the private performance of a great actress to a crowded house of one.

Actors and actresses are apt to act a good deal off the stage; but no one could do it so astonishingly well as E.T. did. Signora Duse was never sure exactly when she was not going to do a little marvel‹ lous acting in a room, and this rendered some of her existence a little difficult—and it was much the same with E.T. Theatre *was* her home, acting her very existence; to act daily, to take a room to be a stage, to make surprising effects, was not only natural to both of them—it was a delight and it was a necessity.

For my part, I never knew where the acting began or left off . . . it was as well not to enquire too curiously.

ARRIVING in the morning or the afternoon, supposing that a son would have the doors opened to him at once, I would be told by one guardian or another to go quietly and quickly— " Hush—hush—sssh "—into the drawing‹room. " SSShhh—be quiet—don't let her hear a sound."

Once, on hearing it was Norman[1] who had called, she had wanted to see Norman—or Bertie,[2] she

---

[1] Norman Forbes.   [2] Sir Albert Seymour.

wanted to see Bertie—if Fred (her brother), she must see Fred—but for some unknown reason her guardians decided it was bad for her health to see any but those whom they decided to bring, thoroughly mystified and not a little furious, into her room. So Norman or Fred or Nellie or Polly were all " hush shsh'ed " off into a passage—into the wings —and told she was far more seriously ill than we could imagine. So we believed this for her sake, and tiptoed away.

This went on a deuce of a time. Even when we got in to see her, there was always a sense of suspense and fear in the room—a strange, harsh voice here or there would rasp out, " Now you're to go to sleep," or " Now you can have dinner," or " You are *not* to go out."

Sometimes, from the next room, where I waited, I would hear her ask in plaintive tones: " Who is it ? " but all the answer she would get would be, " Now go to sleep—it's the postman."

To interfere again, after having already interfered some twenty-odd years previously, at the time of the production of " The Vikings," and learnt what it led to—how it tore her to pieces—was not to be thought of. One had to go away once more, with the rest of her friends, leaving her in the hands of her loving guardians.

III

A ND now came the year 1928. What was it I came over from Italy for? A long journey like that, to an artist who never had any private income, was at all times a rather expensive thing: and in five years I had only been able to get over to England once.

Yes, I remember what it was made it possible. A young couple had recently married, and they were all for my using their flat while they were away— thus making my visit a practical proposition and a pleasant one. And by the help of these friends, I was able to attend my exhibition of designs for "The Pretenders."

It was a great rush, and my mother was down at the Smallhythe Farm, and I was to go down in a week or two. She was apparently pretty well, and up and going around, and now in her eighty-first year.

One day, I seized the opportunity of getting my sister to come up from the country and come along with me to a luncheon-party.

I was awfully glad to see her, and to hear that Mother was pretty fit.

Two days later I got a telephone message from her—" Mother has had a stroke."

This seemed to me one of those impossible things
—inconceivable.

I was soon motoring down to the farm.

I gathered that mother had been left to herself
—and a " companion," and two servants, and two
of my sister's friends—my sister having come up
to town; and that she had somehow eaten something
which she should not have eaten—and after that,
she had this stroke.

I don't much mind *what* it was gave her this damn
stroke—it's the stroke alone which mattered.

A ND there she lay on her bed, all crumpled
up—eyes closed, she could not see with them
—and her face so drawn, all to one side; her lovely
hands as beautiful as in 1880—1890—always—and so
immensely alive and expressive.

Her voice was husky—and she lay murmuring a
good deal. I could not understand what she said—
it was no longer her voice but rather the voice of
some man—more like that of Irving, when murmur‹
ing in the last act of " Louis XI." She was very fallen
—all but the hands, which shone clearly for me,
and seemed to speak.

It is unkind for Nature to strike anyone so fond
of Nature as she was; but then Nature acts and

o

reacts in strange ways—and does not stop to argue long with any. It seems unkinder than it is, I dare well believe.

The doctor I never spoke with. Her brothers and sister came down to see her, but they too did not discuss with the doctor. He was a most attentive and thorough man, but he held out no hope, and said it was a matter of days. She lay still and silent.

ONCE when shifting her, as she lay helplessly on the bed, a touch of the old spirit returned, I was on one side, with my hands under her, the nurses on the other; and on the word "up" we all raised her, the sheet was drawn away and a new sheet put in its place—then, on the word "down," we lowered her. She was very heavy.

But she took up the two words—and played see-saw with them: "Up and down . . . up and down . . ." she growled in a semi-comic, true Terry way. The word *up* went with a sharp jerk, almost like a hiccup but no such thing, and the word *down* went like a heap falling and lengthened out into dowwwn. . . .

Twice she said it, and then—"Up to the skies . . . dowwwwn to the——"—and it tailed away into rumblings.

I tiptoed out into the lane—not convinced I should never hear her say anything else—but these were the last words I heard.

SHE lingered, and the Press representatives came down, because in some lands the chamber of the dying is not respected, if it is a public person who is leaving this great stage of fools.

She died in the morning sun, which shone warm and yellow onto her. She sat up suddenly—opened her eyes—fell back and threw off fifty old years as she fell. She became twenty-five to look at—and in truth, she became once more Nelly Terry, back again at Harpenden with little Edy and little Teddy and the one she loved better than all the world.

ENVOI

LONDONDERRY AIR.

Traditional Irish Melody, harmonized by HENRY G. LEY.

INDEX

INDEX

Readers of this book must not be disappointed to find in it so little about Ellen Terry's countless friends. There would not have been enough space to include them all or all their kindness. I therefore mention only a very few names, and some of these are of people seldom mentioned elsewhere and most are dead.